MY MORNING PRAYER

PRAYER

DEAR LORD, I THANK YOU FOR THIS DAY

BY

DAVID E. QUIEL

Trust in the LORD with all your heart
and lean not on your own understanding;
in all your ways acknowledge Him,
and He will direct your paths.

Proverbs 3: 5-6

Copyrights

Published in the United States of America

Publisher: CreateSpace Independent Publishing Platform (2018)
Language: English
ISBN-13: 978-1986522038
ISBN-10: 1986522032

It is because of my deep love for my Lord and Savior, and His love for me,

that I dedicate this book to my

God

Grandparents

Parents

Sisters

Wife

Children

and

Grandchildren

Inspiration and Influence

I would like to give acknowledgement and recognition to the following individuals who inspired the contents of this book:

Henry Van Dyke
Richard Branson
Reinhold Niebuhr
Terry G. Jones
Harvey Shapiro
Diana Ross
Joel Osteen
Fanny Crosby
Lura Van Wormer Bertram
Keri Wyatt Kent
Jim Cymbala
Glen G. Scorgie
Margaret Feinberg
Elizabeth Peale Allen

Mark & Debra Laaser
Corrie Ten Boom
Stuart Briscoe
Ann Spangler
Tom Holladay
John Burke
John Ortberg
Kevin G. Harney
Brother Yun
Peter Elkblom & Rupert Timpl
T. Scott Daniels
Craig Groeschel
Billy Graham's daughter, Anne
Max Lucado

TABLE OF CONTENTS

PREFACE

"Trust in the Lord with all your heart and lean not on your own understanding; in all your ways acknowledge Him, and He will direct your paths." (*Proverbs 3: 5-6*) This little Bible verse is the story of my life - literally.

This book is a study of my personal prayer to God with an in-depth look at the meaning of each phrase. It is also a Bible study, an educational reference, a reflection on my personal life experiences and my personal talk and walk with Jesus as I continue to build on my relationship with Him. Perhaps this book can also guide you into a deeper relationship with our Savior through the Word of God as you reflect back on your life and look forward to what God has planned for your future. "Your Word is a lamp for my feet, a light on my path." (*Psalm 119:105*)

Reflections

This book is about my walk with Christ with a twist of nostalgia for those that can remember the "good old days". It is a reflection on my life with some disappointments and illnesses along the way to strengthen my faith through God's mercy. It is about how God watches over me physically, mentally, emotionally, financially and spiritually every day, how God has directed my paths, how He has challenged me in my faith, and how He graciously provides for my needs.

I have attempted to capture more than 70 years of my life in a few pages of this preface as a foundation for the many stories and memories in the chapters that follow. You can't buy time or memories. Life is too short. I believe that God has allowed many opportunities and failures to be woven throughout the fabric of my life in order to provide the proper education and foundation necessary for me to have an intimate loving relationship with Him.

I definitely know for a fact that He has a purpose for each day of our lives. Dear Lord, I thank you for each day.

Blessings

God has blessed me in so many ways during my life journey. He could have taken my life at a very early age during a car accident. He could have made me paralyzed for the remainder of my life. He protected me when I was hit by the car and only permitted a hairline skull fracture to remind me of Him. He blessed me with younger twin sisters and loving Christian parents who instilled family values. He blessed me with a respected Christian Pastor and Sunday school to attend and further my education in His Word. He blessed me with the opportunity to attend a Christian parochial school to learn more about Him at a very early age. "For you have been my hope, O Sovereign Lord, my confidence since my youth." (*Psalm 71:5*)

At an early age, He healed my 'physical heart condition' and placed my heart in the middle of my chest to remind me where my heart should always be – God centered. He left a heart murmur (God is always whispering to me) and a right bundle branch block to make sure I listen. "Be still, and know that I am God." (*Psalm 46:10*)

He spoke to me. He watched over me when I was sick with high fevers and pneumonia. He directed my parents to enroll me into a Christian Academy and then directed me in finding financial aid for tuition. He spoke to me a second time and found me full time work. He lovingly reminded me, when I wasn't listening to Him, that it was 'my will' and not 'His will', when He would not let me graduate from college.

He allowed me to experience Guillain-Barre syndrome, which placed me in the hospital, and then He blessed me with a loving wife and three beautiful children. He asked me to share my family values, skills and faith in Sunday School teaching, Church choir, Easter plays, Christmas pageants, outdoor summertime musicals, youth counseling, Cub Scout Master, Boy Scout Leader, Jaycees, coaching soccer, baseball and track, family guitar sing-alongs and camping.

He allowed my job of 37 years to be eliminated, my wife to be chronic depressive and loose the sight of one eye, my father-in-law to lose both legs, my one son to go off to war during Desert Storm and the other son to attempt suicide. He allowed my daughter's best friend to be killed and the terrible terrorist events of September 11th. He guided the surgeon through surgery on my neck and ruptured disks. He gave me patience during each of these stressful times.

Although we were forced to move from our home of more than 27 years, He found a place for us to stay as we waited for His direction. He pointed toward Arizona to provide employment, housing, medical benefits and a new Church home. He gave my wife partial eye sight and eliminated her depression. He allowed me to have severe emphysema and C.O.P.D., but assured me that the nodules and lesions on my lungs were not cancer. He even gave me a light tap on my heart with a mild heart attack to remind me that He is always present in my life.

We continue our lives in Phoenix, and rejoiced at our retirement in 2015 (the same day as our 46th wedding anniversary). He continues to bless us with a loving and caring church family in our retirement. God has made us this promise - "Even to your old age and gray hairs I am He, I am He who will sustain you. I have made you and I will carry you; I will sustain you and I will rescue you." (*Isaiah 46:4*)

God watches over us physically, mentally, financially and spiritually every day! He definitely has a purpose in our lives. That is why I talk with Him every day. He calls me to "press on toward the goal to win the prize for which God has called me heavenward in Christ Jesus." – (*Philippians 3:14*)

Dear Lord, I thank You for each day.

INTRODUCTION
My Morning Prayer

Gratitude

Dear Lord, I thank You for this day. I thank You for giving me the opportunity to see and hear Your Creation this morning. Help me to start this day with a new attitude and plenty of gratitude. Let me make the best of each and every hour to clear my mind so that I can hear from You. Please broaden my mind so I can accept all things.

Blessings And Forgiveness

You have done so much for me and You keep on blessing me. I am truly blessed with God's LOVE! I'm blessed because You are a forgiving God and an understanding God. I ask now for Your forgiveness. Forgive me this day for everything I have done, or may do, say or think that is not pleasing to You. Please keep Your hands on my shoulders to guide me through this day and keep me safe from all danger and harm. Let me not whine and whimper over things I have no control over. And give the best response when I'm pushed beyond my limits.

My Heart

God I love you and I need you. I know that when I can't pray, You listen to my heart. Come into my heart, please! I ask that the Holy Spirit fill my heart with Your love. Father, I want to embrace You with my arms and feel the warmth of Your strong and loving arms around me.

Your Will

Continue to use me to do Your will. Continue to bless me that I may be a blessing to others. Keep me strong that I may help the weak. Keep me uplifted that I may have words of encouragement for others. Remind me to say "Thank You", "I Love You" and "I'm Sorry" as each opportunity arises.

Salvation

I pray for those that are lost and can't find their way. I pray for those that are misjudged and misunderstood. I pray for those who don't know You intimately. I pray for those that don't believe.

Family Values

I believe that God changes people and God changes things. I pray for all my sisters and brothers. For each and every family member in their households. I pray for peace, love and joy in their homes that all their needs are met. I pray that every eye can see there is no problem, circumstance, or situation greater than God. Every battle is in Your hands for You to fight.

Conclusion

I pray that I will continue to receive Your love in my heart and to share this love with every one that I encounter today. In Jesus precious name. Amen!

Pray Daily

Jesus set a fine example for us when talking with our heavenly Father. "Very early in the morning, while it was still dark, Jesus got up, left the house and went off to a solitary place, where He prayed." (*Mark 1:35*)

Although my Lord has taught me to pray daily, I sometimes find myself needing a "jump start", especially in the morning. I have so much to be thankful for, so many blessings, so much of God's love and so much of God's encouragement that I can easily become overwhelmed. That's why I turn to my Lord and Savior. I am excited to begin my day (and ending my day) knowing that God is with me.

8 Second Prayer

Bishop T. D. Jakes is credited with the '8 Second Prayer.'

> *"Lord, I love you and I need you, come into my heart, and bless me, my family, my home, my finances, and all of my friends. In Jesus' name. Amen."*

Well, I could just give God the eight seconds. But, not only am I cheating myself, but I am cheating God of His time He graciously gives me each day, every one of the 86,400 seconds. He taught us to "Pray without ceasing." (*1 Thessalonians 5:17*)

My Morning Prayer

I have seen various versions of morning prayers through the years. A few years ago I decided to enhance the content of these prayers to include my personal thoughts and feelings. I needed many more topics than just *my* love, *my* needs, *my* heart, *my* family, *my* home, *my* finances, and *my* friends that were found in the '8 Second Prayer', and more definition and clarity in my personal life than I had found in other variations.

The Lord's Prayer

Our Lord gave us a great example on how to pray in *Matthew 6:9-13* "This, then, is how you should pray:

> *Our Father in heaven,*
> *hallowed be your name,*
> *your kingdom come,*
> *your will be done,*
> *on earth as it is in heaven.*
> *Give us today our daily bread.*
> *And forgive us our debts,*
> *as we also have forgiven our debtors.*
> *And lead us not into temptation*
> *but deliver us from the evil one.*
> *For Yours is the kingdom and the power and the glory*
> *forever. Amen."*

What a wonderful prayer.

A Conversation With God

How many of us go through our day without talking to God? How is it that we profess to know the Lord Jesus, claiming Him as our friend, yet spend so little time communing with Him in prayer?

Jesus prayed often — at the beginning of His day, before many of His miracles, before His meals, and before and during His crucifixion. He prayed for the lost, for His disciples, for His enemies, for the world, and for Himself. Many of His prayers are recorded in His Word to teach us how to pray, when to pray, and for whom to pray. If Jesus, the perfect Son of God, needed such times with His Father, how much more do we?

Praying is not just reciting a laundry list of needs and desires. Rather, it is listening and paying attention to God in a dialogue with Him. It's discovering where God is at work, and helping Him through your service, giving, and loving. Prayer can strengthen us to do the work that God has called us to do. Prayer is not passive but active. We don't focus on ourselves if we are focused on God.

Max Lucado once said "Our prayers may be awkward. Our attempts may be feeble. But since the power of prayer is in the One who hears it and not in the one who says it, our prayers do make a difference."

Typically, when we run out of things to ask for, we stop praying. If we would talk to God a little longer and listen, He would pour out His heart and mind to us. He would give us invaluable insights into our circumstances. He would counsel us. He would reveal whether we should say 'yes' or 'no' to a present opportunity.

The Proverbs of Solomon emphasize the external religious life. They teach how to practice religion and overcome daily temptations. They express a belief in God and His rule over the universe and, seek to make God the controlling motive in life and conduct. "The Lord is far from the wicked but He hears the prayer of the righteous." (*Proverbs 15:29*)

Six Petitions

With these thoughts of prayer in mind, I offer '*My Morning Prayer*'. This 2 minute prayer actually has six petitions, which I further break down into 32 chapters:

Gratitude	*God's Will*
Blessings and Forgiveness	*Salvation*
My Heart	*Family Values*

I try not to simply read the prayer. As I pray, I pause between each sentence and reflect on the blessings of the previous day – naming them one by one as I remember them. I also reflect on the needs of my sisters and brothers – identifying the specific needs and the specific names of individuals, and on worldly matters – like our government leaders, wars, hunger and education. Sometimes *My Morning Prayer* time is short, while on other days there is so much to say and share that an hour can easily fly by as I talk with God. I also try to take time to listen.

God speaks in a gentle whisper as He did to Elijah. "The Lord said, 'Go out and stand on the mountain in the presence of the Lord, for the Lord is about to pass by.' Then a great and powerful wind tore the mountains apart and shattered the rocks before the Lord, but the Lord was not in the wind. After the wind there was an earthquake, but the Lord was not in the earthquake. After the earthquake came a fire, but the Lord was not in the fire. And after the fire came a gentle whisper." (*1 Kings 19:11-12*)

As I study God's Word, I can usually relate the Bible stories and passages to the petitions contained in *My Morning Prayer*. This assists me in searching God's Word even further. I have found that this prayer is actually an outline that I can use in studying the Word. "The unfolding of your Words gives light; it gives understanding to the simple." (*Psalm 119:130*)

We need God's guidance, and the good news is that He is more than willing to give it if we ask in faith.

God is always at work, finding good for those who love Him. However, God allows unique circumstances into our lives that are highly individualized, such as an accident, lost job, or care for an aging relative. These events are not bad luck. Even though they may be undesirable, our spirituality can grow in new ways to produce qualities of value to God's glory. Our purpose is to see these relationships, moral character, and actions as growth opportunities in our spiritual maturity. "And we know that in all things God works for the good of those who love Him, who have been called according to His purpose." (*Romans 8:28*)

For this reason, I have written this book. Perhaps this book can also guide you into a deeper relationship with our Savior through the Word of God.

PART 1

GRATITUDE

CHAPTER 1-
THANK YOU

DEAR LORD, I THANK YOU FOR THIS DAY.

I have often said that "When you wake up in the morning, stretch out your arms. If you don't feel a casket, it is going to be a great day." Henry Van Dyke once wrote, "Be glad of life, because it gives you the chance to love and to work and to play and to look up at the stars; to be satisfied with your possessions...... to think seldom of your enemies, often of your friends, and every day of Christ; and to spend as much time as you can, with body and with spirit in God's out-of-doors. These are little guideposts on the footpath to peace". And, Paul wrote "Give thanks in all circumstances, for this is God's will for you in Christ Jesus." (*1 Thessalonians 5:18*)

"This is the day the Lord has made; let us rejoice and be glad in it." (Psalm 118:24)

"Enter His gates with thanksgiving and His courts with praise; give thanks to Him and praise His name. For the Lord is good and His love endures forever; His faithfulness continues through all generations." (Psalm 100:4-5)

Today I'm thankful for God's love for me. Every day is a blessing from God. As the psalmist writes "Give thanks to the Lord, call on His name; make known among the nations what He has done. Sing to Him, sing praise to Him; tell of all His wonderful acts. Glory in His holy name; let the hearts of those who seek the Lord rejoice. Look to the Lord and His strength; seek His face always. Remember the wonders He has done, His miracles, and the judgments He pronounced." (*Psalm 105:1-5*)

A.C.T.S.

Years ago I was taught that prayer contained four main petitions:

- *A*doration.

- *C*onfession.

- *T*hanksgiving.

- *S*upplications.

These can be abbreviated as A.C.T.S. First we exclaim adoration to our Creator, then confessing our sins. We thank Him for all of the blessings He has bestowed on us, and finally we humbly ask Him for help. Day by day, minute by minute, we are surrounded by the love of our Lord Jesus Christ and should thank Him with sincere adoration and celebrate each moment.

The Apostle Paul said it perfectly, "Speak to one another with psalms, hymns and spiritual songs. Sing and make music in your heart to the Lord, always giving thanks to God the Father for everything, in the name of our Lord Jesus Christ" (*Ephesians 5:19-20*)

Every day is a new adventure, yearning for our attention. You can have a positive influence on others or a negative effect on them.

"Oh give thanks to the Lord, for He is good, for His steadfast love endures forever!"
(Psalm 107:1)

"Now, our God, we give You thanks, and praise Your glorious name."
(1 chronicles 29:13)

The choice is yours. At the end of the day you can reflect on this:

Finish every day and be done with it.
You have done what you could.

Tomorrow is a new day:
Begin it well and serenely and with too high a spirit
To be cumbered with your old nonsense.

This day is all that is good and fair.
It is too dear, with its hopes and invitations,
To waste a moment on yesterdays.

By Ralph Waldo Emerson

"So then, just as you received Christ Jesus as Lord, continue to live your lives in Him, rooted and built up in Him, strengthened in the faith as you were taught, and overflowing with thankfulness." (Colossians 2:6-7)

Each Day

Sure, there are some days that seem to never end. Stress, regrets and commitments can overwhelm us. And then, there are other days that seem to fly by. For example, seeing an old friend after many years, playing with your children on a day off from work, enjoying your favorite hobby or just spending a quiet day with your spouse. "Always giving thanks to God the Father for everything, in the name of our Lord Jesus Christ." (*Ephesians 5:20*)

Reasons to Thank God

Remember the Gospel story of Jesus healing the 10 lepers (*Luke 17:11-19*)? It's a wonderful recounting of Jesus' generous and healing spirit. Nonetheless, it's a troubling story, because only one of the lepers came back to thank Jesus. How could only one return? How could the other nine dance off in joy, completely forgetting how—and by whom—they were healed?

As Christians, we're called beyond simple thanks for the good things God has sent our way. We're also to give thanks for what He has done for us...and for who He is.

Express Your Gratitude

Elizabeth Peale Allen gives us 10 scriptural reasons to express our gratitude to God for the wonderful gifts He's given us:

1. His love that "endures forever" (*Psalm 107:1*).

2. His grace, freely "given you in Christ Jesus" (*1 Corinthians 1:4*).

3. Continuous victory "through our Lord Jesus Christ" (*1 Corinthians 15:57*).

4. "Righteous laws" to guide us (*Psalm 119:62*).

5. Fellow believers to sustain and cheer us: "I always thank my God as I remember you in my prayers" (*Philemon 1:4*).

6. He has "answered me...[and] become my salvation" (*Psalm 118:21*).

7. He has redeemed us. "While we were still sinners, Christ died for us" (*Romans 5:8*).

8. He has qualified us "to share in the inheritance of the saints in the kingdom of light" (*Colossians 1:12*).

9. "He is good" (*1 Chronicles 16:34*).

10. He is "faithful and just" (*1 John 1:9*).

We need to remember to thank God for each day.

CHAPTER 2 - CREATION

I THANK YOU FOR GIVING ME THE OPPORTUNITY TO SEE AND HEAR YOUR CREATION THIS MORNING.

In the book of Genesis, Moses describes creation …"The Lord God formed the man from the dust of the ground and breathed into his nostrils the breath of life, and the man became a living being." (*Genesis 2:7*) Wow! God gave me life. He created me. He gave me the senses of sight, hearing, touch, smell, taste, speech and "common sense". There is nothing in this universe greater than God and His creation. Every morning I have the opportunity to see and hear His creation.

Laminin Adhesive

A while ago I was watching a YouTube video by Louie Giglio…and I was BLOWN AWAY! He was talking about how inconceivably BIG our God is…how He spoke the universe into being…and, how He breathes stars out of His mouth that are huge raging balls of fire. Then He went on to speak of how this star-breathing, universe creating God ALSO knitted our human bodies together with amazing detail and wonder.

"This is the day that the Lord has made; let us rejoice and be glad in it." (*Psalm 118:24*)

"In the beginning was the Word, and the Word was with God, and the Word was God. He was with God in the beginning. Through Him all things were made; without Him nothing was made that has been made." (*John 1:1-3*)

He then talked about how we can trust that the God who created all this, also has the power to hold it all together when things seem to be falling apart…how our loving Creator is also our sustainer. He then talked about "laminin". Wikipedia describes it as "Laminins are a family of proteins that are an integral part of the structural scaffolding of basement membranes in almost every animal tissue." Laminins are what hold us together….LITERALLY. They are cell adhesion molecules. They are what holds one cell of our bodies to the next cell. Without them, we would literally fall apart.

"God's voice thunders in marvelous ways; He does great things beyond our understanding. He says to the snow, 'Fall on the earth,' and to the rain shower, 'Be a mighty downpour'." (Job 37:5-6)

Thousands of years before the world knew anything about laminin, Paul penned these words. "He is the image of the invisible God, the firstborn over all creation. For by Him all things were created; things in heaven and on earth, visible and invisible, whether thrones or powers or rulers or authorities; all things were created by Him and for Him. He is before all things, and in Him all things HOLD TOGETHER. " *(Colossians 1:15-17)*

"The heavens declare the glory of God; the skies proclaim the work of his hands. Day after day they pour forth speech; night after night they display knowledge." (Psalm 19:1-2)

You can never convince me that this is anything but the mark of a Creator who knew EXACTLY what laminin "glue" would look like long before Adam breathed his first breath! The glue that holds us together - ALL of us - is in the shape of the cross! And we see that from a very LITERAL standpoint, we are held together…one cell to another….by the cross.

When you get a chance, look up "Laminin" on the Internet. Then take a look at some of the images. We carry the cross of Christ in our bodies - it's science!

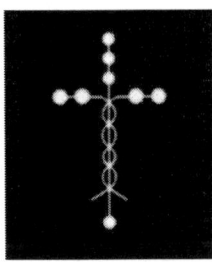

This diagram is of a protein cell found in our bodies called Laminin. This protein HOLDS everything together! This very important cell is in the shape of a cross. Coincidence? I don't think so!

"For everything God created is good, and nothing is to be rejected if it is received with thanksgiving." (1 Timothy 4:4)

In their book *The Laminins* authors Peter Elkblom and Rupert Timpl go into more detail about both the importance of laminins and their structure. They describe laminins that, together with other proteins, "hold cells and tissues together." They also say, "Electron microscopy reveals a cross-like shape for all laminins investigated so far." The strands of laminins do not always stand straight and at right angles, but they do consists of arms, three of which are short and one of which is long.

"As you do not know the path of the wind, or how the body is formed in a mother's womb, so you cannot understand the work of God, the Maker of all things. Light is sweet, and it pleases the eyes to see the sun." (Ecclesiastes 11:5, 7)

The Crown Jewel

God didn't start with the creation of man. In *Genesis 1*, God created stars and land masses, oceans and ecosystems.

He looked at the things he had made and thought to himself, "It is good." Then in *Genesis 2*, He created a human, the crown jewel of His entire creation. God had placed in His beautiful world the one who was meant to become His Son. But then God paused. And for the very first time, when God spoke, He didn't create something new. Looking on the man who shared his breath, God said, "It is not good for the man to be alone. I will make a helper suitable for him." (*Genesis 2:18*).

The First Marriage

I believe that in the Words of creation, we have the Divine appointment of marriage, and also the declaration that the female came after the male, and formed from him. In *Genesis 1:27* and *Genesis 5:2*, the creation of male and female declares "in God's image." The female is described as "a help meet for him:" In the Hebrew it is interpreted as his reflected image. The happiness of marriage is based, not upon the woman being just the same as the man, but upon her being one in whom he sees his image and counterpart. We can make further reference to marriage in *Genesis 3:8* "Then the man and his wife heard the sound of the Lord God as He was walking in the garden in the cool of the day, and they hid from the Lord God."

"The Son is the radiance of God's glory and the exact representation of His being, sustaining all things by His powerful word. After He had provided purification for sins, He sat down at the right hand of the Majesty in heaven." (Hebrews 1:3)

CHAPTER 3 - ATTITUDE

HELP ME TO START THIS DAY WITH A NEW ATTITUDE AND PLENTY OF GRATITUDE.

One of my favorite Bible passages is from Paul in *Philippians 3:14*. "I press on toward the goal to win the prize of God's heavenly calling in Christ Jesus."

My parents enrolled me in Immanuel Lutheran, a private Christian parochial school, in the first grade. This is where my mother had attended as a child. This was a two-room schoolhouse – very cold during the Minnesota winters and very warm during the rainy, humid late springtime. Huge blackboards spanned two walls. We used white chalk on these boards to do our lessons. I hated the screeching sound of the chalk on those boards. We never got a "white slip" or other nonsense for being out of order. Punishment consisted of sitting in a corner or cleaning the erasers.

"Let the message of Christ dwell among you richly as you teach and admonish one another with all wisdom through psalms, hymns, and songs from the Spirit, singing to God with gratitude in your hearts." (Colossians 3:16)

We would walk through a hot and musty basement tunnel, past the boiler room, to eat our lunch in the church basement each day. This is also where we would have choir practice, as well as Bible study and Sunday school classes.

I attended this school off and on until the middle of the 5th grade. In the 4th grade, we moved to a new house on Hampshire Avenue in Golden Valley and I returned to Immanuel parochial school for a brief period of time. The church was constructing a new education building next to the two-room school house. We would often be sidetracked from our lessons as we watched the construction workers. At the end of the 4th grade we were going to have a graduation ceremony. I was excited because I would be able to move into the northern-facing room with the potbelly stove. What a disappointment when I started the 5th grade. The new education building had been completed, and I would be in 'that' building, not the old schoolhouse in the northern room with the potbelly stove. I was very disappointed.

"We Give Thanks ...For each new morning with its light, For rest and shelter of the night, For health and good, for love and friends, For everything thy goodness sends".
- Ralph Waldo Emerson

Good Start To Your Day

It all starts with the right attitude. Wake up in the morning with a great positive attitude and get a good start to your day. We need to know the difference between patience and instant gratification.

The Apostle Paul compares attitude to a race. "Do you not know that in a race all the runners run, but only one gets the prize? Run in such a way as to get the prize." (*1 Corinthians 9:24*) In versus *24-27* the apostle compares himself to the racers and combatants in the Isthmian games, well known by the Corinthians. There is great encouragement to persevere with all our strength. Those who ran in these games were kept on a diet. They exercised. The apostle warned of the dangers in life, and its temptations. Holy fear of himself was needed to keep an apostle faithful. We can learn through humility, to watch against these temptations which surround us while in the body, and start our day with a new attitude so we can say "I have fought the good fight, I have finished the race, I have kept the faith." (*2 Timothy 4:7*)

My parents enrolled me in a private Christian Academy in the 9th grade. The Academy was all male. There were only 40 boys in my class and not more than 200 in the entire Academy. While there, I had the opportunity to manage our track team. As a track manager my responsibilities included setting up equipment such as the hurdles, raking the sand for the long-jump, pacing and encouraging team members as they ran around the track, doing massages when muscles were tight, recording running times with a stopwatch, contacting the media with results of each race and most important was to portray a positive attitude. I even got a "Letter" award for my efforts along with participation on the school yearbook.

Ignore Negativity
Billionaire Richard Branson once said "My attitude has always been, if you fall flat on your face, at least you're moving forward." – after falling flat on his face in a bike accident. Keeping a positive attitude helps for physical, mental and spiritual health. Live your life and ignore the negativity. Don't let anyone steal your happiness. We all have many influences in our lives. Some are positive opportunities, while others are just negative excuses.

Feed Your Faith

Feed your faith with positive thoughts, not the negative. Put all of your energy into positive actions.

Missing somebody?	Call
Want to meet up?	Invite
Want to be understood?	Explain
Have questions?	Ask
Don't like something?	Say it
Like something?	State it
Want something?	Ask for it
Love someone?	Tell them

Those with a negative attitude will respond: "It's not that simple. Sometimes the person you miss won't answer; now what? The one you want to meet up with always has something better to do; now what? The people you want to understand you won't listen; they don't understand what I'm going through because they need to experience it; now what? The people you have questions for, won't listen. Whatever you like, you get criticized for; and if you don't like something, what happens if it doesn't change after you speak up about it? The person you ask something for, won't give it to you; or, you ask politely but still don't get what you asked for? The person you love, doesn't love you back."

We make life difficult by trying to justify our actions or by making excuses for things we do or don't do. Instead, follow the words of Paul, "Therefore, since Christ suffered in His body, arm yourselves also with the same attitude, because he who has suffered in his body is done with sin." (*1 Peter 4:1*)

Examine Yourself

Attitude is everything! There once was a woman who woke up one morning, looked in the mirror, and noticed she had only three hairs on her head. "Well," she said, "I think I'll braid my hair today." So she did and she had a wonderful day. The next day she woke up, looked in the mirror, and saw that she had only two hairs on her head. "Hmm," she said, "I think I'll part my hair down the middle today." So she did and she had a grand day. The next day she woke up, looked in the mirror, and noticed that she had only one hair on her head. "Well," she said, "Today, I'm going to wear my hair in a ponytail." So she did and she had a fun, fun day. The next day she woke up, looked in the mirror, and noticed that there wasn't a single hair on her head. "Wonderful!!" she exclaimed, "I don't have to fix my hair today!!" *Attitude is everything.* "Your attitude should be the same as that of Christ Jesus." (*Philippians 2:5*)

The Mirror

Margaret Feinberg said that through prayer we can discover things about ourselves and God that we could not discover any other way. Prayer provides a mirror to our soul. Through the reflection of prayer, our motives and attitudes are brought to light. Through prayer, we can explore the source of our less-than-becoming behavior. Along the way we discover roots of unforgiveness, agreement with things that simply aren't true, and wounds that go unhealed.

Through prayer, we discover the shadows of our sin and recognize the wonder of God's redemption and restoration. During prayer, our eyes shift from self-focus to God-awareness, and we can find ourselves with a heavenly perspective that is not our own. Looking at life through God's perspective changes everything.

Don't Be Afraid

We are never the answer; Jesus always is. If we do our part, and others do their part, God does His.

Many people are afraid to ask someone to follow Christ. They are afraid no one will respond. You don't fail if the Spirit prompts you to ask someone to follow Christ and the person doesn't. You fail when the Spirit prompts you but you're afraid to ask. Don't blame yourself if someone rejects Jesus. That's putting yourself in God's place.

And don't be tempted to take credit when someone accepts Jesus. "Let the word of Christ dwell in you richly as you teach and admonish one another with all wisdom, and as you sing psalms, hymns and spiritual songs with gratitude in your hearts to God. And whatever you do, whether in word or deed, do it all in the name of the Lord Jesus, giving thanks to God the Father through Him." (*Colossians 3:16-17*)

"For the word of God is living and active. Sharper than any double-edged sword, it penetrates even to dividing soul and spirit, joints and marrow; it judges the thoughts and attitudes of the heart. Nothing in all creation is hidden from God's sight. Everything is uncovered and laid bare before the eyes of Him to whom we must give account." (*Hebrews 4:12-13*)

God can give you strength to overcome anything when you ask Him, let Him and thank Him. We must have faith and believe that God is doing something right now. "You were taught, with regard to your former way of life, to put off your old self, which is being corrupted by its deceitful desires; to be made new in the attitude of your minds;" (*Ephesians 4:22-23*)

Gratitude

Faith, in other words, is thanking God in advance, counting on Him. Gratitude is the quality of being thankful; our readiness to show appreciation for and to return kindness. The Latin word *gratus*, means "pleasing" or "thankful". Gratitude is a feeling of thankfulness. Some synonyms seen in the Bible include: gratefulness, thankfulness, thanks, appreciation, indebtedness, recognition, acknowledgment, and credit. Gratitude is thanking God for what He did, even before it has happened.

Why not set aside some time to increase your "gratitude quotient'?

CHAPTER 4 – EVERY HOUR

LET ME MAKE THE BEST OF EACH AND EVERY HOUR TO CLEAR MY MIND SO THAT I CAN HEAR FROM YOU.

The Bible is a repository of God's past communications. Where God has already spoken is a logical place to look for Him to speak in our lives.

"Then He opened their minds so they could understand the Scriptures."
(Luke 24:45)

Applesauce

A few years ago my wife and I traveled from Phoenix to the Ozarks to listen to our daughter and son-in-law perform at a Bluegrass event. Since our granddaughters were very young, we thought it would be nice to prepare some homemade applesauce for them. All of the jars sealed wonderfully and I packed them tightly in the back of our van for the long trip. It takes two hours to drive from Phoenix to Flagstaff, Arizona, with the elevation climbing from 1100 feet to over 6000 feet surrounded by beautiful mountains.

"Because He turned His ear to me, I will call on Him as long as I live."
(Psalm 116:1-2)

About half way up the mountain we heard a bang, then another. We thought something was wrong with the van. After pulling to the side of the road to investigate, I discovered that the applesauce jars had all broken their seal from the increased elevation. God has a sense of humor. We believe that God was talking to us, clearing our minds for the long trip, and telling us to relax and enjoy His creation.

Confirmation

When I started the 7th grade, I rode the school bus more than 15 miles to Anoka Junior High. I was so excited to begin learning Latin as my required foreign language. We got to learn all about pagan religions, weird gods, myths, dragons and warriors. I believe this is where a seed was planted to understand and appreciate mythology and archeology in Biblical times as I do today.

Reflecting on my studies of Roman mythology, I discovered that we don't need little chubby statutes, holy cows, other weird man-made idols and creations, or reincarnations to be saved. I was able to appreciate how God unselfishly gave us His Son, Jesus Christ, as the only way to our salvation through these first hand experiences. As Christians, all we need to do is to believe in Jesus as Paul writes in *John 3.16*. And in addition to the words of Paul, Jesus Himself tells us "I am the way, and the truth, and the life; no one comes to the Father, but by me." (*John 14:6*)

During the 3rd quarter of the 8th grade, I received membership into the National Junior Honor Society for my academic achievements. (It was a proud moment for my folks.) I was running a 102 degree temperature, but did not want to miss my Confirmation ceremony that evening. I had my mandatory congregational testing of the Lutheran Catechism, required for Confirmation after years of concentrated education from the 5th grade through 8th grade. Both of my parents had been confirmed at Immanuel Lutheran Church. Confirmation is where I testified and rededicated my life to Christ as my Savior. I am happy to say that I was confirmed and also recovered from the fever.

Confirmation in the Lutheran Church was more than a class, it was more than a four year program – it was a ministry where God was active in my life drawing Him closer to my heart. I found that Confirmation helped me feel more at home in the church and taught me ways to be active in the different ministries of the church. Regardless of how old we are, by the grace of God, we continue – each and every day of our lives – to walk our journey of life with God.

For me, Confirmation was more than just memorizing Bible passages and the Lutheran Catechism doctrine. It taught me how my faith could be active in my daily life. It taught me about the promises that God made to me and how I can depend on those promises during my life. Trusting in God isn't just something we hear about, but something we can do ourselves. At the end of the Confirmation program I had a deeper, more personal and honest idea about what I believed, who God is and how to live out that faith in the church and world.

We studied scripture, the sacraments of Baptism, Communion, and the teachings of Martin Luther. We learned through our actions as well as through worship and doing acts of service for others. We had a chance to talk about what we were learning about our faith at home with our parents and at church with our pastor, teachers, and each other.

Confirmation was the beginning of my lifelong journey of faith, filled with new questions and answers, new discoveries, new relationships, new responsibilities, and new possibilities. Confirmation was just one step along a much larger journey of my life. God is with me along the way, each step of the way. Confirmation was a tool that helped me along my life-long adventure of living out my Christian faith.

Listening To God

God wants us to talk to Him, and we want Him to listen. The Psalmist says, "I cried out to God for help; I cried out to God to hear me" (*Psalm 77:1–2*). In addition, God wants us to hear Him: "Give ear and come to Me; hear Me, that your soul may live" (*Isaiah 55:3*).

In order to connect with God, we must talk to Him. We want to know that God hears us, because being heard is a clue that we are fully known. We must talk with God in humility, not through our pride. In fact, the Bible goes so far as to warn us that God hates the sin of pride and will discipline the proud. That is why Scripture says: "God opposes the proud but shows favor to the humble." (James 4:6)

Through silent, attentive listening, the meditative approach to Scripture opens us up to the quiet voice of God. It sets a tone of humility and receptivity, rather than one of assertiveness and control.

Dietrich Bonhoeffer, the German martyr, like many others, commended this approach. He claimed that it was the best way to wait for the Word to address us personally. In *Life Together*, his little classic on Christian community, Bonhoeffer warned against neglecting to listen for the living voice of God. The obscene alternative is just to continue on in God's neglected presence.

CHAPTER 5 - ACCEPTANCE

God Given Talents

I remember doing a "soft shoe" dance to "I'm Forever Blowing Bubbles" at our 5th grade PTA talent show at Riverview Elementary - including red and white striped shirts, wooden canes and straw hats - with three other boys. (This was my first public performance, other than Sunday School Christmas programs.)

During one of our gym classes, in which we were required to learn square dancing, a short little kid, Robert G., stepped on my little toe and broke it. (No – we didn't call the "toe" truck. However, I was in a cast for a long time, trying to hobble onto the school bus using crutches.)

This is also the school where I experienced football. They needed another player, recruited me, suited me up with all the pads and helmet and put me in the game without any instructions.

"Do not conform any longer to the pattern of this world, but be transformed by the renewing of your mind. Then you will be able to test and approve what God's will is— His good, pleasing and perfect will." (Romans 12:2)

"Can all your worries add a single moment to your life?" (Matthew 6:27)

With only one play, I was creamed, did one summersault and sat out the rest of the game.

There was a fireplace in the basement of our house in Brooklyn Park. I would build a nice fire and sit in front of it just reading the Bible or pursuing my interest in drawing and painting. This is where I also learned to play the guitar. I would practice in my grandmother's bedroom, sitting on the little children's chair next to her treadle sewing machine and Grandma would sit on the bedside and play the harmonica.

As part of the music curriculum at Concordia Academy, I learned to play the piano and pipe organ, was a member of the Glee Club choir and went on tours around the United States singing, witnessing and staying with host families along the way. We had even built a harpsichord that we took with, along with guitars and a complete set of heavy-duty risers to stand on.

Each year, we also made a record – one of those 78 rpm vinyl disks that were played on a record player. (One of our classmates copied these albums to CDs for our 50 year class reunion for the Glee Club members.) Our choir also held a musical each year. We would invite our families, relatives and friends. Such productions included "Et tu Brute" and "Susanswerphone."

"All things have been committed to Me by my Father. No one knows the Son except the Father, and no one knows the Father except the Son and those to whom the Son chooses to reveal him."
(Matthew 11:27)

"This is what the Lord says, He who made the earth, the Lord who formed it and established it— the Lord is His name: 'Call to Me and I will answer you and tell you great and unsearchable things you do not know.'"
(Jeremiah 33:2-3)

Noah's Ark

Everything I need to know, I learned from Noah's Ark.

1. Don't miss the boat.

2. Remember that we are all in the same boat!

3. Plan ahead. It wasn't raining when Noah built the Ark.

4. Stay fit. When you're 60 years old, someone may ask you to do something really big.

5. Don't listen to critics; just get on with the job that needs to be done.

6. Build your future on high ground.

7. For safety's sake, travel in pairs.

8. Speed isn't always an advantage. The snails were on board with the cheetahs.

9. When you're stressed, float awhile.

10. Remember, the Ark was built by amateurs; the Titanic by professionals.

11. No matter the storm, when you are with God, there's always a rainbow waiting.

Radio Dilemma

I remained in a parochial school until the middle of the 5th grade. My folks bought a new house with a walk-out basement in the northern suburb of Brooklyn Park near the Mississippi River. Transportation into the city each day became difficult, so I was enrolled in a public school again. I finally got to ride a school bus up the River Road for the first time to Riverview Elementary.

It was in this house where I became very interested in electricity. My dad had a radio in the garage that was not working.

I sat on the cement steps in front of the house in my shorts on a hot summer afternoon, took the case off of the radio, placed the metal chassis on my bare legs and plugged it in. (I will never forget that tingling experience that could have electrocuted me.) I built a workshop in the basement, purchased a vacuum tube tester, and began fixing all the radios and T.V.'s in the neighborhood.

One of my classmates, David N., lived in a house near the Mississippi River. We spent many summer days building a tree house on a vacant lot next to his house. I remember tent camping in his front yard. He had one of the original battery-operated transistor radios that had both AM and FM. He played this the entire night until the battery died. He slept very well, but I stayed awake the entire night listening to that radio.

Put Your Heart In The Right Place

After multiple tests, the doctors determined that I had a heart condition called WPW syndrome. This is an abbreviation for the Wolff-Parkinson-White syndrome, a condition caused by an abnormality in the electrical system of the heart which normally tells the heart muscle when to contract. In the WPW syndrome, there is an extra electrical connection inside the heart that acts as a short circuit, causing the heart to beat too rapidly and sometimes in an irregular manner. In later years, this condition disappeared. The doctors had also told me that they determined that my heart was not on the left of my chest, it was in the middle. (Did that mean that my heart wasn't in the right place with God?) I also have a right bundle branch block in the heart muscle and a heart murmur from birth.

Ignore Critics

Life is too short to worry about what others say or think about you. So just enjoy life, have fun, and give them something to talk about. Not everyone is going to accept you and understand you. Social media, work, your friends and neighbors cause all kinds of distractions just trying to influence you. You find bullies and critics everywhere. Don't let negative people bait you – ignore them. To reach your potential, don't be offended by others. Embrace your potential.

Take a lesson from Mordecai in the book of *Esther*. He never grew weary. God rewarded him and punished Haman for trying to destroy the reputation of Mordecai. You need to let God defend you. Learn to ignore your critics who challenge your reputation and focus on your goals. David had an urgent plea to God for help in trouble, to defend him and to let him keep his focus in *Psalm 69*.

Be Aware

For religion classes at Concordia Academy, our professor taught us how to give 10 minute sermonettes in the chapel based on his selected verses from the Bible. He would say, "Tell them what you are going to say, say it in three points, and then tell them what you said."

This reminded me of the story of the elderly lady that sat in the first pew in church, right below the pulpit. The new Pastor started his sermon with "I come...". He couldn't remember what he was going to say next. He remembered, however, what his professor taught him, "Begin the statement again." So he repeated "I come...". He again could not remember. So he decided to try once more. On saying "I come..." the third time with great enthusiasm, he fell out of the pulpit onto the lap of the elderly lady. Upon apologizing, she responded "After the first two warnings, I should have moved."

Serenity Prayer

The Serenity Prayer is the common name for an originally untitled prayer, most commonly attributed to the theologian Reinhold Niebuhr. The prayer has been adopted by Alcoholics Anonymous and other twelve-step programs. While Niebuhr's authorship was once believed to be secure, *Yale Book of Quotations* editor Fred R. Shapiro in 2008 published evidence that puts elements of Niebuhr's claim in doubt and shows that a version of the prayer was in existence no later than 1936.

According to the most common attribution, Reinhold Niebuhr wrote the prayer for use in a sermon, perhaps as early as 1934. He is quoted in the January, 1950 *Grapevine* as saying the prayer "may have been spooking around for years, even centuries, but I don't think so. I honestly do believe that I wrote it myself."

Reinhold Niebuhr's versions of the prayer were always printed as a single prose sentence; printings that set out the prayer as three lines of verse modify the author's original version.

The Serenity Prayer

God grant me the serenity
to accept the things I cannot change;
courage to change the things I can;
and wisdom to know the difference.

Living one day at a time;
Enjoying one moment at a time;
Accepting hardships as the pathway to peace;
Taking, as He did, this sinful world
as it is, not as I would have it;
Trusting that He will make all things right
if I surrender to His Will;
That I may be reasonably happy in this life
and supremely happy with Him
Forever in the next.
Amen.

--Reinhold Niebuhr

Shapiro suggests that Niebuhr most likely unconsciously adapted the prayer from existing formulations of unknown origin, although he acknowledges the possibility that Niebuhr introduced the prayer by the mid-1930s in an unpublished or private setting.

"God grant me the serenity to accept the things I cannot change; courage to change the things I can; and wisdom to know the difference." Through this prayer, we are encouraged to accept all things with the help of God.

PART 2

BLESSINGS AND FORGIVENESS

CHAPTER 6 - BLESSINGS

The Concordia Academy campus had its own chapel (twice a day), a separate administration and classroom building, cafeteria building, large library building, a music building, science building and several dormitories. This was both an Academy and College campus where I would be spending the next 8 years, prior to going to seminary.

In 2015 we had an opportunity to go back to Minnesota for my 50-year class reunion. We took a tour of the campus where I spent more than 7 years. I stood in the area called "The Knoll" just reminiscing about the "good old days". This was a park-like area of trees right behind our Academy dormitory. We were able to walk through the tunnel that joined our dormitory to the Administration building. I even had the opportunity to take pictures of the old books in the library where I polished the floors as one of my part-time jobs.

"If you fully obey the Lord your God and carefully follow all His commands I give you today, the Lord your God will set you high above all the nations on earth. All these blessings will come upon you and accompany you if you obey the Lord your God."
(Deuteronomy 28:1-2)

This was the same campus that my Uncle Leroy had attended. He became a Lutheran minister after graduating from this school. (I used to enjoy listening to his English and German sermons when we went to visit his rural congregations in southern Minnesota.) I admired him so much. He had extra talents working with wood – for example, making an organ out of an accordion and duplicating and replacing a broken claw leg on a pedestal table.

Jealousy

Sometimes we may fall into the trap of looking at the success of others, yearning for a better life, greater fortune or more talents. This has often been called "keeping up with the Jones's." Jealousy comes from counting others blessings instead of our own.

Expectations

We need to take inventory of the many gifts and blessings that God has given us. But, we must also be aware of our limitations, ability and suitability for each task that He may assign to us.

Stuart Briscoe said that we can turn to prayer as a 'declaration of dependence' — a heartfelt cry to God for these gifts. Prayer must be a litany of longing.

"Blessed is the man who finds wisdom, the man who gains understanding, for she is more profitable than silver and yields better returns than gold. She is more precious than rubies; nothing you desire can compare with her. Long life is in her right hand; in her left hand are riches and honor. Her ways are pleasant ways, and all her paths are peace. She is a tree of life to those who embrace her; those who lay hold of her will be blessed." *(Proverbs 3:13-18)*

The promise of overflowing blessings is made in the book of *John* to those who are "thirsty" — those who in recognition of their own needs are willing to freely confess them, are eager to address them, and are ready to take whatever steps will release the promised provision. (*John 7:37-38*) On the last and greatest day of the Feast, Jesus stood and said in a loud voice, "If anyone is thirsty, let him come to Me and drink. Whoever believes in Me, as the Scripture has said, streams of living water will flow from within him."

Prayer must also be an expression of expectation — a humble claiming of the unchanging promise of blessings made by the Son of God. This is an assurance that the promised Spirit is resident in us and is ready to accomplish what He has been sent in and through obedient, dependent servants.

Count Your Blessings

God has blessed me with the opportunity to learn about Him and how to apply this in my life. He has showered me daily with His gifts. Pray, not because you need something, but because you have a lot to thank God for. Let's examine some examples of blessings.

My wife had a tap on her heart in July of 2011. The doctors found a 95% blockage that they were able to open up with a stent. Praise Our Lord!

"Every good and perfect gift is from above, coming down from the Father of lights with whom there is no variation or shadow due to change."
(James 1:17)

"We give thanks to God always for you all, constantly mentioning you in our prayers, remembering before our God and Father your work of faith and labor of love and steadfastness of hope in our Lord Jesus Christ."
(1 Thessalonians 1:2-3)

Although she is blind in her right eye, the Lord blessed her with a surprise. After 12 years of blindness in her right eye, we were directed to see an eye specialist and he was able to fit her with a prosthetic eye. During January 2015, she received a temporary fitting. It is similar to a very large contact lens that looks very real. All of her eye muscles still function, so she can move the prosthetic eye left, right, up, down, blink and open/close. The final custom-made eye was hand-painted to match her other eye and was ready in March 2015.

While she volunteered at a MOPS group (Mothers Of Pre-Schoolers) a few years ago, a little 6 year old boy named Caleb in her class told her that "one day Jesus will come and give you an eye." She didn't think it would ever be possible, but all things are possible through God. Praise His name! With partial sight in her left eye, my wife can still do some tasks.

Corrie Ten Boom wrote "In the concentration camp I lived near a crematorium for months. I was living in the shadow of death. I did not know beforehand that they would release me a week before they would kill all the women my age. It was a human error and a miracle of God. When you face eternity, and that was what was happening to me, you see everything so clearly. Here I was weak and sinful, and there was the Devil, much stronger than me, much, much stronger than me. But there was Jesus, much, much stronger than the Devil. And together with Him, I was more than a conqueror."

Johnson Oatman, Jr., born April 21, 1856, was a citizen of Lumberton, N.J. His dad was a local merchant and was the best singer in town, with a rich, powerful voice. Young Johnson could not sing as well as his father, yet he grew up wanting to make some musical contributions of his own. For a time, he worked in the family business, but soon began to study for the ministry. After finishing school and ministering in the Methodist Episcopal churches, he continued to hope that life held some other plans for him.

At 36, he realized that he had a musical talent to write songs for other Christians to sing. He eventually had written 5,000 songs and was happy that in his musical compositions he had found a way to "preach the Gospel."

One of the most notable is the hymn called "Count Your Blessings". The chorus goes like this:

Count your blessings, name them one by one.
Count your blessings, see what God has done.
Count your blessings, name them one by one.
Count your many blessings see what God has done.

Remember to count your blessings every day.

CHAPTER 7 - LOVE

I AM TRULY BLESSED WITH GOD'S LOVE!

God loves us so much that He already has made plans for our life. "For I know the plans I have for you,' declares the Lord, 'plans to prosper you and not to harm you, plans to give you hope and a future." (*Jeremiah 29:11*)

Did you know there's a book about you? God wrote it before you were conceived in your mother's womb: "You saw me before I was born. Every day of my life was recorded in your book. Every moment was laid out before a single day had passed." (*Psalm 139:16*)

"We know and rely on the love God has for us. God is love. Whoever lives in love lives in God, and God in him. We should also love as God has taught us". (1 John 4:16)

God has set the goals, but it's up to us to discover what's recorded for our lives through prayer, reading His Word, and other spiritual means. Then, by His grace, we can fulfill them. God created you to fulfill specific purposes. Identify your talents, skills, and desires.

Then think and pray about them, asking God to reveal His purposes to you and give you a clear sense of your calling.

Surrender

Don't block God's best for you by withholding a part of yourself from Him. If you surrender to God, He will bless you by revealing more of His will to you and acting to bring about good in your life. Know that God's timing is perfect. When things go right for you, thank God and give Him the glory.

"Then celebrate the Feast of Weeks to the Lord your God by giving a freewill offering in proportion to the blessings the Lord your God has given you." (Deuteronomy 16:10)

Be truly open to whatever plans He may have for you. Understand that obstacles may be tests from God designed to strengthen your faith. Know that God will use the past, present, and future to work in your life in a providential way, weaving all things together for good purposes. Pay attention to doors He opens and those He closes.

"Love is patient, love is kind. It does not envy, it does not boast, it is not proud." (1 Corinthians 13:4)

God cares about every detail of your life and wants to guide you through it. He is willing to reveal His wisdom to you for all decisions – both minor (attending an event) and major (such as whether you should marry the person you're dating).

I was admitted to the hospital and diagnosed with Guillain-Barre (pronounced: ghee-yan bah-ray) syndrome, sometimes called French Polio.

This is a rare medical condition that affects the nerves outside a person's brain and spinal cord. Although the condition can be frightening because it often causes people to have some type of paralysis, Guillain-Barre syndrome is very rare. It only affects one or two people in every 100,000. Most of the people who do get Guillain-Barre syndrome recover and are able to return to their normal lives and activities. The only issue is that I can never get a flu shot.

"Yet the Lord set His affection on your forefathers and loved them, and He chose you, their descendants, above all the nations, as it is today." (Deuteronomy 10:15)

Acceptance

While suffering from this Guillain-Barre as a patient in the hospital, I met a Nurses Aid. She gave the best back rubs. She started visiting me during her off hours. The Chart Nurse finally forbid her to see me. So, when I finally left the hospital, the only natural thing to do was to take her on a date.

It was August. (To this day, she still says we never went on a date. I would just call her up and tell her what time I would be there.) After several 'dates', we made a trip to meet her parents. They lived on a dairy farm in northern Minnesota. It was on one of many weekends that, while sitting in the car watching shooting stars near a northern Minnesota lake, we talked about aspirations, marriage, children and religion.

I was raised Lutheran, she was raised Baptist. We had both accepted Christ into our lives at a young age and agreed that our family would someday follow *Joshua 24:15* – "Choose for yourselves this day whom you will serve ... as for me and my household, we will serve the Lord."

In late October of 1968, she came with me to an art museum with my 5th grade Sunday School class. That evening we went to dinner in Somerset, Wisconsin where I asked her to be my wife. We drove to my folks' house to announce the engagement, and then drove 2 hours north so that I could ask for her fathers' blessing. God surely blessed me with wonderful in-laws.

"The Lord appeared to us in the past, saying: "I have loved you with an everlasting love; I have drawn you with unfailing kindness." (Jeremiah 31:3)

"Follow God's example, therefore, as dearly loved children and walk in the way of love, just as Christ loved us and gave Himself up for us as a fragrant offering and sacrifice to God." (Ephesians 5:1-2)

We were married on March 1, 1969 in the same Church where I became a Christian. This is where we made our commitment "To have and to hold, from this day forward, for better or for worse, for richer or for poorer, in sickness and in health, to love and to cherish, till death us do part." What a wonderful blessing and milestone we can celebrate together each year!

We renewed these vows on our 40th wedding anniversary at the Troon North Golf Club in Scottsdale Arizona after I submitted and won a radio contest. During these past years we have experienced many roller coaster rides, and continue our marriage journey as best friends. Our marriage vows have permeated our lives from broken bones to heart attacks, through good days and bad. It is with God's continuous love, protection, guidance and direction that we can continue our journey together to support and love each other daily. I LOVE YOU DEAR.

"Who shall separate us from the love of Christ? Shall trouble or hardship or persecution or famine or nakedness or danger or sword? As it is written: 'For your sake we face death all day long; we are considered as sheep to be slaughtered.' No, in all these things we are more than conquerors through Him who loved us." (Romans 8:35-37)

Raising A Family

What is on the table is never as important as who is around it.

My wife and I were blessed with three children. In 1970, after our first son was born, we decided to purchase our first house. Like many young couples, we thought we knew what we were doing financially. But after one year, we couldn't make the $125 mortgage payments. We decided to become landlords, renting our house to strangers in order to make the mortgage payments, and then we could rent a townhouse. We found a young couple with one child to rent our property. After two months of defaulting on their rent, we were forced to evict them. We also found out they were using our house for hashish drug distribution. My wife was pregnant with our second child. By this time we were now in default on the mortgage, forced to give the house back to the bank.

We moved into the basement of my folk's house. What an embarrassment. Our second son was born in 1972, during the time we were living there. We had made a kitchenette to do our own cooking near the fireplace in the basement. I remember coming home with groceries and, for some reason, a bottle of syrup dropped and splashed onto the fireplace brick. That was a real mess to clean up. Another time, upon lighting a fire with fresh logs stored outside, we found ourselves fighting millions of ants as they came scurrying out of the burning logs.

After getting back on our feet, we were finally able to move into our own apartment and later into another townhouse. On a 20 degree below zero morning that Minnesota winter in 1976, our daughter was born.

As parents, we volunteered for many activities. These included Sunday School teaching, Church choir, Easter plays, Christmas pageants, outdoor summertime musical, youth counseling, Cub Scout Master, Boy Scout Leader, Jaycees, coaching soccer, baseball and track. In our spare time we loved family guitar sing-alongs and camping. We always did things as a family. Now they are all grown up, married, and have children of their own.

As a Scout leader, we had decided on a winter sledding at Boone Hill. This was actually two hills with a path between them. During the winter months in Minnesota, the city would plow a path in the snow between the hills and neighbor kids could slide down the hills.

We owned a toboggan. I asked my three children to wax the toboggan before we got to the hill to make sure it would be fast enough. Since I was the leader, I was chosen to go down the hill first, with my two boys. We went really fast until we hit the snowbank created by the plow. We were told that our toboggan and cargo went twenty feet in the air. Upon landing and laughing, I found that my eye glasses had gotten lodged into my left eyebrow. Quick trip to the emergency room and a few stitches.

I remember the 1991 Halloween storm where we got 37 inches of snow in less than a two day period in Minneapolis. My wife and I were in Florida for a business convention, leaving our teenagers home. It was 75 degrees when we left the Minneapolis airport and 85 degrees in Florida. We had only packed summer clothes. On returning to the Minneapolis airport, I had parked on the top level of the parking ramp. With wearing only a short sleeve shirt, I had to scrape the snow and ice off of the car.

It usually took 40 minutes to drive from the airport to our home in Brooklyn Park. This trip took two and a half hours, driving on deep ice ruts on the highway. When we got home we found that the driveway had not been shoveled. Our children gave the excuse that the snow blower wouldn't start. I guess that shovels weren't invented yet.

Personal Passions
I love my wife, I love my children and I have always had a passion for chocolate. It must have been from the Easter when my Aunt Lil gave me a huge Easter basket of chocolate rabbits. I love

raised chocolate-glazed doughnuts as well, and I especially love Boston Cream Pie with the chocolate glaze as my birthday cake. Mom used to make that cake every year for my birthday. On my 7th birthday, we invited some of my friends to my birthday party. Unfortunately I was unable to attend because I got the chicken pox.

Healing Words

When you tell someone, "I love you", "I'm proud of you", or "you did a great job on that project", you're not just being kind, those are healing words. We don't know what people are going through. They may smile on the outside, but on the inside they're hurting, they're lonely, they're insecure. Just a simple word of encouragement, "I'm praying for you." Or a simple compliment, "You look great today" can be what keeps them moving forward.

We are here for one reason. To love each other the way God loves us. If you don't know Him, just open your heart and welcome Him in and He will embrace you with a love you have never known before. "You are loved more than you will ever know by someone who died to know you." (*Romans 5:8*)

CHAPTER 8 - UNDERSTANDING

I'M BLESSED BECAUSE YOU ARE A FORGIVING GOD AND AN UNDERSTANDING GOD.

After graduation from the Academy, many of the young men went to different colleges; some went into the military service, some into nursing, others into legal, and several into teaching or mission work. I came back to the same campus, enrolled as a Ministerial College student along with several of my Academy classmates. Even though I had been on this campus for the past four years, I really hadn't been exposed to the college girls on the same campus, much less in the same classes. (A new frontier!)

Sacrifices

I didn't really appreciate the sacrifices that my parents made, financially, to put me through the Academy. After my first year of college, my parents could no long afford the tuition, forcing me to get a job or two.

"God saved us, not because of the good things we did, but because of His mercy".
(Titus 3:5)

"I always thank my God for you because of His grace given you in Christ Jesus. For in Him you have been enriched in every way - with all kinds of speech and with all knowledge "(1 Corinthians 1:4-5)

I worked part time as a stock boy at a department store on weekends, campus cafeteria for breakfast and supper, campus janitorial work in the evenings, washing and buffing the hallways and library floors, and then I rounded out the night by walking the campus hallways on security duty.

That paid my tuition for the first two quarters of my second year. But, as the funds started to dwindle, and lack of sleep caught up with me, God spoke to me as he had done once before. He said "Go into the world." (Now who is going to argue with God?)

Going Into The World

I put my college education on hold and landed a full time job working for a large electric utility company. It was an office job, folding blueprints for the construction workers. During this time, I volunteered to be a Sunday School teacher for 5th graders. (They are like a sponge for learning new things.)

I also had many opportunities to share my faith at work and, after one year, I had saved enough money that I was able to quit my full time job and go back to school. But this time I hadn't talked to God, I just assumed that this is what He wanted me to do. (Well let me tell you, make sure you validate your decisions with Him before you move on with your life independently).

Since I had not saved enough money for both tuition and campus dormitory fees, I commuted from home each day during the first two quarters of my 3rd year of college.

Disappointment

The President of the college called me into his office. He said that, since I was unable to take gym classes due to my "heart condition called WPW syndrome", he would allow me to take whatever classes I wanted at his college as part of a teacher curriculum, but I would never be able to graduate, since the State had strict laws about education requiring that all students must take physical education. I sure didn't see that coming. I switched to the teacher curriculum the following quarter and completed the required student teacher assignment at an elementary school 2nd grade class near our home in Brooklyn Park.

I had forgotten that God said "Go into the world." My own will and passions had gotten in the way of God's plan for my life. (*Jeremiah 29:11*) After considering the tuition fees and never being able to graduate, I decided to withdraw from college.

Career Path

I returned to my previous employer, tail between my legs, and asked for my old job back. Silly me, I didn't expect that they would have filled my position after only six month. But, my previous Supervisor had an idea. He set up an interview with the Chief Electrical Engineer to fill a position as a draftsman.

During the interview, they asked if I knew anything about electricity. (Boy, did I have experience in that area, especially with the radio on my lap on that hot summer afternoon.) They also asked if I had any drafting experience and I said yes. (I had 10 weeks of drafting in 7th grade shop class.) I stayed in that job for more than 10 years. (I stayed with the same company for more than thirty-seven years, exploring other career paths such as records management, computer technologies, and learning seven different programming languages.)

Earthly Nature

Consider God's imperfect heroes. The talent pool has always been pretty thin when it comes to moral perfection. Noah got drunk. Abraham lied about his wife. Jacob was a deceiver. Moses murdered an Egyptian. Rahab was a harlot. Samson had serious problems with lust and anger. David was an adulterer. Paul persecuted the church. Peter denied Christ.

If God chose only well-rounded people with no character flaws, some of the credit would inevitably go to the people and not to the Lord. By choosing flawed people with a bad past, a shaky present, and an uncertain future, God alone gets the glory when they accomplish amazing things by His power. Turn your life over to Jesus Christ.

There is hardly any public person in America today who has not exemplified the "earthly nature" ("flesh" in the King James and the literal Greek) that Paul urges the *Colossians* to shed: "Put to death, therefore, whatever belongs to your earthly nature: sexual immorality, impurity, lust, evil desires and greed, which is idolatry." (*Colossians 3:5*). Idolatry, greed, and sexual immorality are intertwined in individual lives and whole societies. Sexuality is designed to be properly ordered within marriage, a relationship marked by covenant faithfulness and profound self-giving and sacrifice. To indulge in sexual immorality is to make oneself and one's desires an idol.

God's Grace
King David began with a reliance on God who called him from the sheepfold to the kingship, and by the grace of God it did not end with his exploitation of Bathsheba and Uriah. The Lord sent His Word by the prophet Nathan to denounce David's actions.

Many Christian leaders who could have spoken such prophetic confrontation to Him personally have failed to do so. David quickly and deeply repented, leaving behind the astonishing and universally applicable lament of his own sin in *Psalm 51*. And the biblical narrative leaves no doubt that David's sin had vast and terrible consequences for his own family dynasty and for his nation. God works in mysterious ways and we do not always understand.

CHAPTER 9 - ASKING

I ASK NOW FOR YOUR FORGIVENESS.

If I ask for forgiveness, what's in it for me? When we confess our sins and repent, Peter tells us of a great gift from God - "Repent and be baptized, every one of you, in the name of Jesus Christ for the forgiveness of your sins. And you will receive the gift of the Holy Spirit". (*Acts 2:38*)

"Do not be anxious about anything, but in every situation, by prayer and petition, with thanksgiving, present your requests to God. And the peace of God, which transcends all understanding, will guard your hearts and your minds in Christ Jesus." (Philippians 4:6-7)

Statute Of Limitations

There is no "statute of limitations" on sin. Many people don't feel the need to confess their sins to God. Your relationship with God is weakened when you try to hide sin from Him. In *1 John 1:8* we find these word, "If we claim to be without sin, we deceive ourselves and the truth is not in us."

Any obstacles you put in the way of your relationship with Him remain there until you take action to remove them. Solomon gives us clear instruction regarding our actions. "He who conceals his sins does not prosper, but whoever confesses and renounces them finds mercy. Blessed is the man who always fears the Lord, but he who hardens his heart falls into trouble." - (*Proverbs 28: 13-14*) When you confess what you've done and sincerely ask for God's forgiveness, your relationship with God heals.

The Mercy Connection

His mercy is not based on our performance. If it were only dependent on us living a perfect life, none of us would be here. That's the beauty of mercy.

Without His forgiveness, our lives would be hopeless because our connection with God would be broken forever. Sin breaks that connection. Because of God's great compassion and His desire to restore our connection to Him, He graciously extends forgiveness to anyone who asks and who is also willing to extend it to others.

Anne Spangler once said "I started thinking about how I had responded during the early months of the Iraq war when Saddam Hussein's two sons were killed. "Yes!" Both times, my response was instinctive, like cheering for my favorite football team. But then a discomfiting thought crept in. Was Jesus rejoicing at the death of these two men? I turned back to the Scriptures in *Luke 6:37*. "Do not condemn, and you will not be condemned. Forgive, and you will be forgiven. If you forgive others when they sin against you, your heavenly Father will also forgive you. How many times should you forgive? Seventy-seven times." These were Jesus' words. But really, I have to forgive rapists and mass murderers? This Jesus, He asks so much. Yes, but He gives so much. "Let your face shine on your servant; save me in your unfailing love." (*Psalm 31:16*)

When you admit your failings and open yourself to God's forgiveness, you can feel His mercy. When you see how gracious God has been, you will feel more willing to pray for a change of heart. Instead of cheering the demise of those men in Iraq, Ann wanted the grace to forgive as she had been forgiven, to let pure justice remain where it belongs — in God's hand.

Self-Illusions

Forgiveness is a process. It begins when you decide to forgive. But it can take time to let go of your emotional reactions to what someone has done and your desire to see them suffer for it. But

God doesn't have emotional reactions. His forgiveness happens instantly — the moment you repent.

What a positive thing repentance is. The Greek word that often translates "repentance" in the New Testament is METANOIA. It expresses the idea of turning, of doing an about-face, of heading away from one thing so you can head toward another. It's not just a turning away from the disintegrating power of sin but a turning toward the creative, life-giving power of God. It's choosing to stand in the light rather than to linger in the darkness.

We don't like having our weaknesses exposed. We find it hard to look squarely into our heart, to have our self-illusions punctured. Perhaps by slowing down and allowing yourself to feel the pain, not to wallow in it, you will be given the grace to recognize what led to your failures. Maybe God will give you not only His forgiveness but the kind of self-understanding that will help you break out of the habits and patterns that lead to sin. Receiving God's forgiveness is a process rather than an event.

Cleansing

How do you sincerely ask God for forgiveness? David has given us a beautiful prayer starting in *Psalm 51:1*: "Have mercy on me, O God, according to your unfailing love; according to Your great compassion blot out my transgressions. Wash away all my iniquity and cleanse me from my sin. For I know my transgressions, and my sin is always before me. "

"Against You, You only, have I sinned and done what is evil in Your sight, so that You are proved right when You speak and justified when You judge. Surely I was sinful at birth, sinful from the time my mother conceived me. Surely You desire truth in the inner parts; You teach me wisdom in the inmost place. Cleanse me with hyssop, and I will be clean; wash me, and I will be whiter than snow."

"Let me hear joy and gladness; let the bones You have crushed rejoice. Hide Your face from my sins and blot out all my iniquity."

"Create in me a pure heart, O God, and renew a steadfast spirit within me. Do not cast me from Your presence or take Your Holy Spirit from me. Restore to me the joy of Your salvation and grant me a willing spirit, to sustain me."

"Then I will teach transgressors Your ways, and sinners will turn back to You. Save me from bloodguilt, O God, the God who saves me, and my tongue will sing of Your righteousness. O Lord, open my lips, and my mouth will declare Your praise. You do not delight in sacrifice, or I would bring it; You do not take pleasure in burnt offerings. The sacrifices of God are a broken spirit; a broken and contrite heart, O God, You will not despise." *(Psalm 51:1-17)*

CHAPTER 10 -
PLEASING

FORGIVE ME THIS DAY FOR EVERYTHING I HAVE DONE, OR MAY DO, SAY OR THINK THAT IS NOT PLEASING TO YOU.

When we celebrate Easter - the death, resurrection and ascension of our Lord Jesus Christ - remember that Christ carried His cross to bear our sins.

Humility

In *Philippians 2:8* we find "And being found in human form, He humbled Himself by becoming obedient to the point of death, even death on a cross. .... Let us fix our eyes on Jesus, the pioneer and perfecter of our faith, who for the joy set before Him endured the cross, scorning its shame, and sat down at the right hand of the throne of God."

"Christ Bearing the Cross" is an oil painting by artist Nicolaos Tzafouris (Greek, ca. 1455–1500/1501).

"May the words of my mouth and the meditation of my heart be pleasing in Your sight, O Lord, my Rock and my Redeemer."
(Psalm 19:14)

"For the LORD takes delight in his people; he crowns the humble with salvation."
(Psalm 149:4)

This Renaissance painting abounds with representations of Christ bearing the cross on the road to Calvary, either as an isolated figure, or with an executioner assailing Him, or accompanied by soldiers, curious bystanders and followers, among whom the depiction of Simon of Cyrene is relatively common.

Christ carrying the cross on His way to His crucifixion is an episode included in all four Gospels, and a very common subject in art. The episode is mentioned, without much detail, in all the canonical Gospels: *Matthew 27:31–33, Mark 15:20–22, Luke 23:26–32* and *John 19:16–18*. From rejoicing during Palm Sunday, to the time that Pilate sentences Christ, to the crucifixion, only John specifically says Jesus carried His cross, and all but John include Simon of Cyrene, who was recruited by the soldiers from the crowd to carry or help carry the cross.

Trespasses
Besides you, who else knows what you REALLY think? Take a look at The Lord's Prayer in *Matthew 6:14-15*. Jesus gives a wonderful example of repentance.

> *"And forgive us our trespasses, as
> we forgive those who trespass
> against us.
> And lead us not into temptation,
> but deliver us from evil."*

"Since we have these promises, dear friends, let us purify ourselves from everything that contaminates body and spirit, perfecting holiness out of reverence for God."
(2 Corinthians 7:1)

"This will take place on the day when God will judge men's secrets through Jesus Christ, as my gospel declares."
(Romans 2:16)

"If we confess our sins, He is faithful and just and will forgive us our sins and purify us from all unrighteousness."
(1 John 1:9)

Lord, please forgive me for any wrong-doing or sin. If you forgive individuals for their trespasses, your heavenly Father will also forgive you. But, if you don't forgive them, your Father will not forgive your trespasses.

Walk In The Light

God is not our puppet. His grace does not give us license to live however we want. He expects our devotion and submission to His Word.

If we choose to persist in sin, we have no assurance that God will bless us. God wants His children to "walk in the light, as He is in the light" (*1 John 1:7*). This is not meant to be perfection, but the willingness to be transparent and sincere with God. It also means repenting when God points out our disobedience, as He did to the nation of Israel at Gilgal in *Joshua 5:2-9*.

"The Lord detests the thoughts of the wicked, but those of the pure are pleasing to him." (Romans 7:14-25)

"Dear children, do not let anyone lead you astray. He who does what is right is righteous, just as He is righteous. He who does what is sinful is of the devil, because the devil has been sinning from the beginning. The reason the Son of God appeared was to destroy the devil's work." (1 John 3:7-8)

The Sinners Prayer

The Sinner's Prayer (also called the Consecration Prayer and Salvation Prayer) is an evangelical Christian term referring to any prayer of repentance, prayed by individuals who feel convicted of the presence of sin in their lives and have the desire to form or renew a personal relationship with God through Jesus Christ.

While some Christians see reciting the sinner's prayer as the moment defining one's salvation, others see it as a beginning step of one's lifelong faith journey. It also may be prayed as an act of "re-commitment" for those who are already believers in the faith.

Often, during or at the end of a worship service, in what is known as an altar call, a minister or other worship leader will invite those desiring to receive Christ (thus becoming born again) to repeat with him or her the words of some form of a sinner's prayer. It also is frequently found on printed gospel tracts, urging people to "repeat these words from the bottom of your heart".

"For you were once darkness, but now you are light in the Lord. Live as children of light (for the fruit of the light consists in all goodness, righteousness and truth) and find out what pleases the Lord." (Ephesians 5:8-10)

The "Sinner's Prayer" takes various forms. Since it is considered a matter of one's personal will, it can be prayed silently, aloud, read from a suggested model, or repeated after someone modeling the prayer role. There is no formula or specific words considered essential, although it usually contains an admission of sin and a petition asking that Jesus enter into the person's heart. It is sometimes uttered by Christians seeking redemption or reaffirming their faith in Christ during a crisis or disaster, when death may be imminent.

Reverend Billy Graham offered this version of The Sinners Prayer:

> *"Dear Lord Jesus, I know that I am a sinner, and I ask for Your forgiveness. I believe You died for my sins and rose from the dead. I turn from my sins and invite You to come into my heart and life. I want to trust and follow You as my Lord and Savior. In Your Name. - Amen."*

"Do not be afraid," Samuel replied. "You have done all this evil; yet do not turn away from the Lord, but serve the Lord with all your heart." (1 Samuel 12:20)

"Dear friends, do not believe every spirit, but test the spirits to see whether they are from God, because many false prophets have gone out into the world." (1 John 4:1)

CHAPTER 11 - GUIDANCE

We had a small luggage tag hung from the visor of our vehicle. We received this on Father's Day from our church in Minnesota just a month before we moved to Arizona. It reads:

"Trust in the Lord with all your heart and lean not on your own understanding;

in all your ways acknowledge Him, and He will direct your paths, "
(Proverbs 3:5-6)

Direction

Oh Lord, give me clarification everyday as You taught me in *Psalm 119:64*, "The earth is filled with Your love, O Lord; teach me Your decrees."

"By day the Lord directs His love, at night His song is with me— a prayer to the God of my life."
(Psalm 42:8)

"The Lord is my strength and my shield; my heart trusts in him, and I am helped. My heart leaps for joy and I will give thanks to him in song."
(Psalm 28:7)

God was with us during the entire 1,800 mile trip in our little 4 cylinder S10 Dodge pickup on the way to Phoenix to start a new chapter in our lives. He protected us. He guided us. He kept us on the right path. He showed us His great creation, the beauty of the flat plains, the hillsides and the mountaintops. On a different return trip back from Minnesota, He also showed us His power and the devastation that can be caused from tornadoes as they literally wipe out entire towns.

"And David shepherded them with integrity of heart; with skillful hands he led them." (Psalm 78:72)

When we arrived in Phoenix, Arizona, He found a house for us to rent and new church home just blocks away. We were able to get medical insurance through my employer. As a result, my wife had five eye surgeries, and although she finally went blind in the right eye, the surgeon, through God's guidance, was able to spare the left eye. We praised the Lord as David said in *Psalm 146:8* "The Lord gives sight to the blind." My company allowed me to work out of a home office, so I was able to assist my wife with recovery from each of the surgeries.

"I know, O Lord, that a man's life is not his own; it is not for man to direct his steps." (Jeremiah 10:23)

GPS Navigation

You may be familiar with several popular GPS navigation systems such as Magellan, TomTom, Google Maps, MapQuest or Garmin that operate on satellite signals. These are designed to give very specific and detailed instructions once you provide your destination,

"'I know the plans I have for you,' declares the Lord, 'plans to prosper you and not to harm you, plans to give you hope and a future.'" (Jeremiah 29:11)

showing a route overview, giving you step by step directions, and informing you when you will be arriving at your location.

On one of our return trips from Minnesota, we had asked our old Garmin (we named her "Dizzy Lizzy") to locate a restaurant in Albuquerque, New Mexico. (The maps in this device had not been updated for a long time.) She provided several suggestions. After arriving at the first location, it had been closed for a long time. The second route brought us through a dark alley that led to nowhere, and finally the Garmin identified the Owl Cafe on old Rt 66.

We had purchased a new Garmin that had lifetime updates to maps for a separate trip to the Ozarks. On returning from the Ozark mountains in Arkansas, we encountered a lot of fog. The navigation satellite kept changing our directions until we were finally lost. We had to rely on a small gas station employee to get us going again.

Unlike a GPS, God may give us instructions for our lifelong journey, but He doesn't give details. We must trust in Him!

The Academy

I continued my studies of Latin, and the other stuff too, well into the 9th grade, until one day my parents came and took me out of public school in Anoka, Minnesota.

"For He has not despised or disdained the suffering of the afflicted one; He has not hidden His face from him but has listened to his cry for help."
(Psalm 22:24)

"Direct my footsteps according to Your word; let no sin rule over me."
(Psalm 119:133)

"Who shall separate us from the love of Christ? Shall trouble or hardship or persecution or famine or nakedness or danger or sword?"
(Romans 8:35)

We drove to a different school in St. Paul. (Not that this was surprising based on our previous moves.) Well, this time it was different! They enrolled me in a private Christian Academy, dormitory room and everything. I was enrolled to become a Lutheran Minister at Concordia Academy at 275 North Syndicate! Mr. Treichel was the Dean.

"If the Lord delights in a man's way, he makes his steps firm; though he stumble, he will not fall, for the Lord upholds him with his hand." (Psalm 37:23-24)

God had directed my parents to enroll me in this school. I would begin intense learning of the Bible in King James English, and eight years of Bible study in Latin, German, Hebrew and Greek. We were taught how to read and write these languages, not really speak them in a conversation. I would learn many Bible facts and, in religion class, memorize Romans Chapter 8 in its entirety.

Those four years in the Academy were wonderful. My science professor was a fascinating man. "Observe and Explain" was his mantra. I had Professor P. W. Stor through all four years of the Academy, as well as three years of College, just as my Uncle had studied. He taught biology and chemistry, but more than that, he taught me life lessons like respect and honesty. He had a great memory, remembering my uncle, and still had all of my uncle's assignments tucked into his small corridor of an office that the students lovingly referred to as the 'Stor' room. I was very fortunate to be his chemistry lab assistant during my college courses.

My math professor was also an innovative instructor. He taught us math, algebra, geometry, trigonometry, calculus, astronomy and physics. I was like a sponge, drawing on his every lesson, especially the wonders of God's creation - the universe, stars and planets.

Our Walk With God
There is an old hymn that reminds me of God guiding me through each day and keeping me safe from harm that was inspired

by this Bible verse: "For though He was crucified through weakness, yet He lives by the power of God. For we also are weak in Him, but we shall live with Him by the power of God toward you." (*2 Corinthians 13:4*)

Just a Closer Walk with Thee

I am weak, but Thou art strong;
Jesus, keep me from all wrong;
I'll be satisfied as long
As I walk, let me walk close to Thee.

Refrain:
Just a closer walk with Thee,
Grant it, Jesus, is my plea,
Daily walking close to Thee,
Let it be, dear Lord, let it be.

Through this world of toil and snares,
If I falter, Lord, who cares?
Who with me my burden shares?
None but Thee, dear Lord, none but Thee.

When my feeble life is o'er,
Time for me will be no more;
Guide me gently, safely o'er
To Thy kingdom shore, to Thy shore.

The word "*walk*" appears some 388 times in its various forms in the New King James Version of the Bible. Many of those occurrences do not have reference to the physical act of walking, but of one's conduct. Considering that, one cannot help but understand that the Word of God places a great deal of emphasis upon how one ought to live.

Many Bible characters were commended for walking with God, such as, Enoch (*Genesis 5:22-24*), Noah (*Genesis 6:9*), Abraham (*Genesis 17:1*), and David (*1 Kings. 9:4*). In *Amos 3:3* the question is asked, "Can two walk together, unless they are agreed?" Since the obvious answer to that is "no," then we learn that to "walk with God" means to be in total agreement with God.

Just as those in the days of old walked with God, so should we. "…And what does the Lord require of you but to do justly, to love mercy, and to walk humbly with your God?" (*Micah 6:8*) We should daily strive to walk more closely to God. The Bible declares, "Draw Near To God, and He will draw near to you" (*James 4:8*). That can be accomplished by daily Bible study (*2 Timothy 2:15*), prayer (*Luke 18:1*), and seeking the kingdom (*Matthew 6:33*).

There are four wonderful blessings to be gained by a closer walk with God contained in the lyrics of that marvelous old hymn, *Just A Closer Walk With Thee* – power, protection, provision and peace.

Wonderful Blessings

Power. The first words of the hymn confess, *"I am weak but Thou art strong."* The Psalmist was keenly aware of his own weakness and dependence upon God's strength in his life. "Have mercy on me, O Lord, for I am weak..." (*Psalm 6:2*). "God is our refuge and strength, a very present help in trouble" (*Psalm 46:1*).

The Apostle Paul boldly proclaimed, "I can do all things through Christ who strengthens me" (*Philippians 4:13*). He reminded young Timothy that "God has not given us a spirit of fear, but of power and of love and of a sound mind" (*2 Timothy 1:7*). We must always remember that we are weak but God will empower us to do His work on earth. "Finally, my brethren, be strong in the Lord and in the power of His might" (*Ephesians 6:10*).

Protection. The hymn continues, *"Jesus keep me from all wrong."* Among the most comforting words in the entire Bible are those found in *Psalm 23:4*. "Yea, though I walk through the valley of the shadow of death, I will fear no evil; For You are with me;

Your rod and Your staff, they comfort me." A closer walk with God will assure His divine care and protection over us.

Provision. *"I'll be satisfied as long as I walk close to Thee."* God is able to satisfy every need that we have, whether physical or spiritual. David made a wonderfully profound observation when he said, "I have been young, and now am old; yet I have not seen the righteous forsaken, nor his descendants begging bread" (*Psalm 37:25*). Those who walk close to God will daily enjoy His wonderful provisions.

Peace. *"Guide me to that peaceful shore."* The sorrows and tribulations of this world can be overcome only by a closer walk with God. The Bible says, "Be anxious for nothing, but in everything by prayer and supplication, with thanksgiving, let your requests be made known to God; and the peace of God, which surpasses all understanding, will guard your hearts and minds through Christ Jesus" (*Philippians 4:6-7*). Determine that you will strive to walk more closely to God, "and the God of peace will be with you." (*Philippians 4:9*)

"The overwhelming multitudes of this world are walking hand in hand with the devil down the broad and easy way that leads to eternal destruction (Matthew 7:13). However, an eternal home in heaven is in store for all who seek just a closer walk with Thee!" - Terry G. Jones

He gives us direction every day. "This is what the Lord says— your Redeemer, the Holy One of Israel: 'I am the Lord your God, who teaches you what is best for you, who directs you in the way you should go.'" (*Isaiah 48:17*)

CHAPTER 12 - WHINING

LET ME NOT WHINE AND WHIMPER OVER THINGS I HAVE NO CONTROL OVER.

My Space

My grandmother's birthday was on New Year Day. Every year we would invite the relatives to celebrate her birthday. There was always a large feast in the dining room. Since I was a slow eater, I was always teased that I would still be eating dinner at breakfast the next morning.

After the meal, the ladies would gather in the living room and the guys would take over my bedroom to watch the football game. My bedroom was very small with wood paneling. Dad would bring the TV into my room and the guys would sit on my bed and smoke their cigars during the game. I hated that smell, even to this day. It would take weeks to air out that room.

"Yet I am always with You; You hold me by my right hand. You guide me with Your counsel, and afterward You will take me into glory." (Psalm 73:23-24)

Hanging On

I spent a summer on a Wyoming ranch with one of my classmates and his family after graduation. This is where I learned how to ride a horse, ride into the mountains for a round-up, sleep under the stars, drive the heard down to the ranch and then the art of branding. Fields were divided by irrigation canals, and manually flooded to water crops periodically. I especially remember the Palomino horse named "Old Paint". She was a beautiful horse with tan and white markings. This is the horse that I first learned to saddle and to ride.

On one of my solo adventures, I took her about 2 miles in back of the ranch at a slow walk, and would occasionally progress to a trot in order to learn how to pace my posterior with the saddle. After about a half hour, I decided to return to the ranch since it was nearing dinner time. This horse knew the way home. She started into a gallop, and all I could do was hang on. Then, very unexpectedly, she abruptly stopped at the irrigation canal, while I continued across the canal through the air and landed in the cactus. She continued back to the ranch on her on. I, on the other hand, was forced to walk back with cactus needles in my posterior. As I leaned over the edge of the kitchen sink, my friends' dad, Wil, pulled each needle out with a pliers.

"Do everything without grumbling or arguing, so that you may become blameless and pure, "children of God without fault in a warped and crooked generation. Then you will shine among them like stars in the sky as you hold firmly to the word of life. And then I will be able to boast on the day of Christ that I did not run or labor in vain." (Philippians 2:14-16)

Running Away

When I was about 6 or 7 years old, my mother demanded my sisters and me to go upstairs and take a nap. Of course I thought I was too old for such nonsense. I was whining and complaining all the way up the stairs. Being the 'big' brother, my sisters followed my poor example. Once upstairs, we began to plan our escape. We decided to run away from home. We found some short sticks taken from a doll bed, tied some doll blankets to the ends, and loaded them with some of our possessions.

As we were sneaking down the stairs, our Grandmother spied us. Instead of stopping us and forcing us back upstairs, she simply asked a question. "What do you plan on eating when you leave home?" We hadn't thought about that. She then made a suggestion. If we could wait a few minutes, she would gladly make us peanut butter sandwiches to take along. We gladly waited and then said our goodbyes. Once outside, we couldn't decide where to go. So, we sat on the front steps, ate our dry peanut butter sandwiches (Grandma didn't put any butter on the dried up bread slices), and decided that maybe taking a nap wasn't such a bad idea.

Have you ever felt like running away or hiding because you didn't get your own way? Have you ever run away or hid from God like Adam and Eve did in the Garden Of Eden because you were tempted or ashamed? *Genesis 3:8* "Then the man and his wife heard the sound of the Lord God as He was walking in the garden in the cool of the day, and they hid from the Lord God among the trees of the garden."

Garden Of Eden

So, where was the Garden Of Eden? There is so much to learn about early civilizations. *Genesis 2:10–14* lists four rivers in association with the garden of Eden: Pishon, Gihon, the Tigris, and the Euphrates. It also refers to the land of Cush—translated/interpreted as Ethiopia, but thought by some to equate to Cossaea, a Greek name for the land of the Kassites.

Legend has it that the Kush (or Cush) were the oldest race on earth and Nubia is regarded by some as the location of the Garden of Eden.

"Thus says the Lord: "The wealth of Egypt and the merchandise of Cush, and the Sabeans, men of stature, shall come over to you and be yours; they shall follow you; they shall come over in chains and bow down to you. They will plead with you, saying: 'Surely God is in you, and there is no other, no god besides him.'" (Isaiah 45:14)

Kush was a civilization centered in the North African region of Nubia, located in what is today northern Sudan. It is one of the earliest civilizations to develop in the Nile River Valley. As a rich trading culture, it lived for centuries at peace with neighbors due to its role in commerce and in the transportation of goods. Their Pharaohs have been called the 'Black Pharaohs', or the 'Ethiopian Pharaohs'. The Kush are referenced in the Bible and were known to the Romans.

Egyptians began moving south, and it is through them that most of our knowledge of Kush comes. The Egyptians prevailed, and the region became a colony of Egypt under the control of Thutmose I. Although ruled by foreigners from about 1500 until about 780 B.C.E. the people of Kush greatly benefited from their physical location on important trade routes.

Women played a key role within the governance of the kingdom, almost unique in the ancient world. A succession of female rulers in Kush represents an 'innovation not seen in any other major civilization' (with the exception, perhaps, of the Hittites).

"The name of the second river is the Gihon. It is the one that flowed around the whole land of Cush." (Genesis 2:13)

"Cush fathered Nimrod; he was the first on earth to be a mighty man." (Genesis 10:8)

"Miriam and Aaron spoke against Moses because of the Cushite woman whom he had married, for he had married a Cushite woman." (Numbers 12:1)

Women In the Bible

There are 140 women mentioned by name and 93 who speak in the Bible. There are 56 women who appear in Scripture who face a crisis which changes the course of their lives, and sometimes their nation's life.

These women in the Bible represent every phase of any woman in the world. They range in age from the young (Mary, the mother of Jesus at 15; Jephthah's daughter at about the same age), to the very old (Sarah, birthing Isaac at 90). Among them are virgins, wives, daughters, slaves, harlots, widows, orphans, single women, married, mothers, barren, three Queens, one Judge, patriots, leaders, victims of rape, prostitutes and those of political power. Some are in parables while others are in teaching stories.

There are anywhere between 200 to 400 women, appearing in the Hebrew Scriptures, the New Testament, the Deuterocanonical books and the Apocryphal books. There are unnamed women identified, usually attached to a husband, son, territory or event.

Even Goddesses, though not "real' women, affected the fidelity of Israel to the one and only God. It was by suffering the consequences of her repeated infidelity that Israel, repentant and restored, was grounded, once and for all, in the truth of Moses. (*Deuteronomy 6:4*)

Don't Get Discouraged

Sometimes we lose our motivation, whine or complain, and just give up. There will be times where you have to stand strong and fight the good fight of faith. In *Matthew 11:30* Jesus said, "My yoke is easy and My burden is light." He was saying you're going to go through times of struggle, strain and difficulty but don't get discouraged, it's not permanent.

The Bible teaches us, "Do everything without complaining or arguing, so that you may become blameless and pure, children of God without fault in a crooked and depraved generation, in which you shine like stars in the universe as you hold out the word of life—in order that I may boast on the day of Christ that I did not run or labor for nothing." (*Philippians 2:14-16*)

The P.L.O.M. Disease

Make reference to *Psalm 101:4* as you read this little story about the P.L.O.M. disease: There was a girl who was a chronic complainer. Even when opportunity knocked, she grumbled about the noise. One day her mother had heard enough of her complaints and said to her, "You've got a bad case of P. L. O. M. disease. That means Poor Little Ole Me." Self-pity! It doesn't help, it hinders. It doesn't lift, it lowers. It doesn't purify, it poisons. Self-pity will parch your attitudes, paralyze your abilities, and put off your achievements. It prohibits excellence and prevents expansion. Let's say with the Psalmist, "I will reject all selfishness and stay away from every evil." (*Psalm 101:4*)

The wandering Israelites had no control over their situation, yet they whined and complained to Moses too. They were camped on the border of the Promised Land, but acted like spoiled brats. (*Numbers 21:4-5*) "But the people grew impatient on the way; they spoke against God and against Moses, and said, 'Why have you brought us up out of Egypt to die in the desert? There is no bread! There is no water! And we detest this miserable food!'" God had all the grumbling He could take, so He sent fiery snakes among the people, and they bit the people; and many of the people of Israel died.

After they repented, God instructed Moses to create a bronze serpent and put it on a pole. If a snake bit them, all they had to do was look at this bronze serpent and live.

We don't have a bronze serpent to look at when we have our temper tantrums. Instead, God has given us Christ to look at.

CHAPTER 13 - RESPONSE

Admission

During one of those quiet times during Kindergarten, someone tossed a winter cap across the room. I soon found out that it was my cap. The teacher told the class that we would all have to remain in the class, even after school, until someone admitted to the crime. Since it was my cap, and I wanted to go home, I chose to volunteer for the crime. I never did find out who the culprit was.

Close Call

During the winter of 1953, on the 1st of February, an uninsured driver hit me as I crossed the street while walking home from school in the 1st grade. (The police report said that I was thrown more than 75 feet into someone's yard on the opposite corner of the intersection.) I can still remember looking for my Hopalong Cassidy lunch box and the Police Officer asking me where I lived - and then bringing me home to our Knox Avenue house.

"My dear brothers, take note of this: Everyone should be quick to listen, slow to speak and slow to become angry," (James 1:19)

"Do not let any unwholesome talk come out of your mouths, but only what is helpful for building others up according to their needs, that it may benefit those who listen." (Ephesians 4:29)

My mother answered the door. (They tell me that my face was all bloody.) My grandmother tended to 'cleaning me up', while my mother called for the ambulance. I was in the hospital for an entire week. The doctors determined that I had a hairline fracture on the back of my skull. My winter clothing, including the heavy duty red plaid lumberjack cap with earflaps, is what the doctors said saved me. (I now know it was God's angels protecting me.)

I just wanted to get out of the hospital because my birthday was on February 7th. They discharged me on my birthday and sent me home with balloons and a chocolate birthday cake with white frosting and yellow flowers that the nurses had provided.

My normal bedroom was upstairs shared with my sisters, but my parents didn't want me to walk up and down the stairs so they put me in 'their' main floor bedroom.

I remained home for more than two months. The other first graders in my class, along with all the other grades in our school, had made cards for me. My parents' bedroom looked pretty neat, all decorated with the cards. Different students would bring me homework each night so that I could keep up with the studies.

"When you are brought before synagogues, rulers and authorities, do not worry about how you will defend yourselves or what you will say, for the Holy Spirit will teach you at that time what you should say."
(Luke 12:11-12)

"When they hurled their insults at him, he did not retaliate; when he suffered, he made no threats. Instead, he entrusted himself to Him who judges justly."
(1 Peter 2:23)

Prop Me Up

When asked to pray, think of the old deacon who always prayed, 'Lord, prop us up on our leanin' side.' After hearing him pray that prayer many times, someone asked him why he prayed that prayer so fervently.

He answered, 'Well sir, you see, it's like this... I got an old barn out back. It's been there a long time; it's withstood a lot of weather; it's gone through a lot of storms, and it's stood for many years.

It's still standing. But one day I noticed it was leaning to one side a bit. So I went and got some pine poles and propped it up on its leaning side so it wouldn't fall. Then I got to thinking about how much I was like that old barn. I've been around a long time. I've withstood a lot of life's storms. I've withstood a lot of bad weather in life, I've withstood a lot of hard times, and I'm still standing too.

But I find myself leaning to one side from time to time, so I like to ask the Lord to prop us up on our leaning side, 'cause I figure a lot of us get to leaning at times.

Sometimes we get to leaning toward anger, leaning toward bitterness, leaning toward hatred, leaning toward cussing, leaning toward a lot of things that we shouldn't. So we need to pray, 'Lord, prop us up on our leaning side', so we will stand straight and tall again, to glorify the Lord."

PART 3

MY HEART

CHAPTER 14 - NEED

GOD I LOVE YOU AND I NEED YOU.

God's greatest command is "Love". (*Deuteronomy 6:5, Mark 12:30, Matthew 22:37* and *Luke 10:27*)

What is "love"? The Apostle Paul tells us that "Love is patient, love is kind. It does not envy, it does not boast, it is not proud. It does not dishonor others, it is not self-seeking. It is not easily angered. It keeps no record of wrongs. Love does not delight in evil but rejoices with the truth. It always protects, always trusts, always hopes, and always perseveres. Love never fails. But where there are prophecies, they will cease; where there are tongues, they will be stilled; where there is knowledge, it will pass away." (*1 Corinthians 13:4-8*)

"Love the Lord your God with all your heart and with all your soul and with all your strength." (*Deuteronomy 6:5*)

"Love the Lord your God with all your heart and with all your soul and with all your mind and with all your strength." (*Mark 12:30*)

Commitments And Feelings

You may give someone a Valentine's Day card or give a gift to show your feelings. Or, you may make a commitment to someone, an engagement proposal, or even marriage. There are several types of commitments and feelings of love.

I remember the children's' gospel song:

> *Jesus loves me this I know*
> *For the Bible tells me so*
> *Little ones to him belong*
> *They are weak but he is strong*
> *Yes Jesus loves me*
> *Yes Jesus loves me*
> *Yes Jesus loves me for the Bible tells me so.*

I yearn to continuously have that kind of love for my God. The love that Jesus has for His children. The love that we have for our children. The love that our parents have for us.

(This command is also found in Matthew 22:37 and Luke 10:27.)

"Within your temple, O God, we meditate on your unfailing love." (Psalm 48:9)

"Because of the Lord's great love we are not consumed, for his compassions never fail. They are new every morning; great is your faithfulness." (Lamentations 3:22-23)

English is a fascinating language. The dictionary has only 3 entries to describe this single word called "love":

As a noun

1. An intense feeling of deep affection. "babies fill parents with intense feelings of love". Synonyms include deep affection, fondness, tenderness, warmth, intimacy, attachment, and endearment.

2. A person or thing that one loves. "she was the love of his life" Synonyms include beloved, loved one, love of one's life, dear, dearest, darling, sweetheart, sweet, angel, and honey.

As a verb

1. Feeling a deep romantic or sexual attachment. "Do you love me?" Synonyms include care very much for, feel deep affection for, hold very dear, adore, think the world of, be devoted to, idolize, and worship.

"And I pray that you, being rooted and established in love, may have power, together with all the Lord's holy people, to grasp how wide and long and high and deep is the love of Christ, and to know this love that surpasses knowledge that you may be filled to the measure of all the fullness of God."
(Ephesians 3:17b-19)

With seven years in the Academy and College studying the Bible in Latin, German, Hebrew and Greek, I found that, unlike the single English word 'love", there are very specific words in both the Old and New Testaments that have been translated as "love" in English. And, each translation of "love" also has a range of meanings. The Bible also distinguishes between commitment-love and feeling-love.

This chapter is an educational overview of the word "love" in both the old and new testaments to give you a better understanding of the various kinds of love and how we are really saying "*God, I love you and I need You.*"

We are commanded to have *agape* love (*Matthew 5:44*) but not *phileo* love because feelings cannot be commanded. *Phileo* is also the word for "kiss." Jesus asked Peter if he had unconditional, sacrificial *agape* love, but Peter responded that he had *phileo*, or brotherly love. Peter's love deepened, and he wrote of *agape* love in his later books.

What kind of love do you have for God?

"For God so loved the world that he gave his one and only Son, that whoever believes in him shall not perish but have eternal life." (John 3:16)

"See what great love the Father has lavished on us, that we should be called children of God! And that is what we are! The reason the world does not know us is that it did not know him." (1 John 3:1)

"Israel, put your hope in the Lord, for with the Lord is unfailing love and with him is full redemption." (Psalm 130:7)

Old Testament Love

Biblical Hebrew is primarily a verbal language. Without trying to teach you Hebrew grammar in this book, let me simply explain that verbs (as well as nouns) are derived from "roots." In Hebrew, verbs are combined to reflect their tense and mood, as well as to agree with their subjects in gender, number, and person. Each verb has an inherent voice.

The ending of verbs may have various inflections. For example: "I would love to go to the movie with you", or "I love chocolate doughnuts" or "I love you Grandma" or "I love my new puppy". The usual word set for "love" in the Hebrew Bible is the verb אהב ('āhēb) in its various inflections (Qal, Piel, Niphal, Pealal, and Hiphil) and its similar nouns 'ahab, 'ōhab, and 'ahebāh (אהבה). The range of possible meanings of אהב ('āhēb) includes "to like" as well as "to love".

There are 12 Hebrew words that have been rendered "love" in the Bible, some are related, some are very common, and some are rather rare.

For instance, רעיה (ra'yāh) occurs only in Solomon's *Song of Songs* with reference to a "female companion, girlfriend, beloved". The *Song of Solomon* is a series of lyrical poems organized as a lengthy dialogue between a young woman and her lover. A third party, or chorus, occasionally addresses the lovers. The first poem is spoken by the young maiden, who longs to be near her lover and enjoy his kisses. Solomon is portrayed as great in wisdom, wealth and power beyond either of the previous kings of the country, but also as a king who sinned. His sins included idolatry, marrying foreign women and, ultimately, turning away from Yahweh, and they led to the kingdom being torn in two during the reign of his son Rehoboam.

Less rare in some verses in the Song of Songs is דוד (dōd) beloved, lover; in other verses in the *Song of Songs*, as well as in a couple of verses in *Ezekiel* and in one verse in *Proverbs*, the word means "love (lust)".

One of the rarest words for love in the Hebrew Bible is חבב (khōbēb), which occurs only in *Deuteronomy 33:3*. "Surely it is you who love the people; all the holy ones are in your hand. At your feet they all bow down, and from you receive instruction." This text speaks of God loving the people. God truly loved the people; all His saints, קדשיו (kedoshaiv), the people whom He had consecrated to Himself, under His special benediction; in order to make them a holy nation.

God had displayed His glory on Mount Sinai, where the people had fallen prostrate at His feet with humble adoration, sincerely promising the most affectionate obedience. God had commanded them a law which was to be the possession and inheritance of the children of Jacob. This law, though delivered with fire and smoke and thunder, which might seem to be hatred and terror, in truth was given to Israel, in great love, as being the great mean of their temporal and eternal salvation.

Also rare (occurring only in *Jeremiah* and in *Ezekiel*) is the verb עגב (plural participle = 'ōgebīm): to desire sensuously. From the same original word or root of עגב (occurring only in *Ezekiel*) is עגבה '(agābāh) meaning passion. *Ezekiel 16:8* "'Later I passed by, and when I looked at you and saw that you were old enough for love, I spread the corner of my garment over you and covered your naked body. I gave you my solemn oath and entered into a covenant with you, declares the Sovereign Lord, and you became mine." Two separate visits are spoken of here: the one in Israel's infancy in Egypt, when God blessed and multiplied her (*Ezekiel 16:6*); the other when she had become a nation, and God entered into covenant with her in the Exodus and at Sinai. The verse describes this covenant in terms of the marriage relation, a figure very frequent in Scripture.

Another rare word is ידי (yādīd) —Beloved —Adjective lovely; a related word that only has one instance of use is recorded

ידידות (yedīdōt) = love (song) *Psalm 45:1.* "My heart is stirred by a noble theme as I recite my verses for the king; my tongue is the pen of a skillful writer", rendered "wedding" (song) in some versions. This psalm or poem was composed by David under divine inspiration. David is speaking of the King Messiah; the King of the whole world, over whom He reigns in a spiritual manner, and in righteousness.

The Qal inflection of the verb רחם occurs once in the Hebrew Bible meaning to love *Psalm 18:2* "The Lord is my rock, my fortress and my deliverer; my God is my rock, in whom I take refuge. He is my shield and the horn of my salvation, my stronghold." Those that truly love God, may triumph in Him as their Rock and Refuge, and may call upon Him with confidence. There are quite a number of occurrences of the same verb in the Piel inflection meaning to greet (meet) someone with love, take pity on someone. There are five occurrences in *Hosea* and one in *Proverbs* in which the Pual inflection of the verb means to find mercy. Hosea is believed to be the first prophet to use marriage as a metaphor of the covenant between God and Israel, and he influenced latter prophets such as Jeremiah. He is among the first writing prophets, and the last chapter of *Hosea* has a format similar to wisdom literature.

Then there is the most variously rendered word in the Hebrew Bible (there are nearly as many different renderings as there are English versions): חסד (khesed). Here is the range of possible meanings of the word:

- Joint obligation between relatives, friends, host and guest, master and servant; closeness, solidarity, loyalty; lasting loyalty, faithfulness, protection favor of the king.

- חסד in God's relationship with the people or an individual faithfulness, goodness, graciousness

- Plural, the individual actions resulting from solidarity: of people, godly action, achievements, proof of mercy

Note that the word "love" does not appear in the range of possible meanings above; however, the words "love", "loving", and "loving-kindness" are quite prominent in English renderings of חסד (khesed):

Loving [חסד (khesed)] *Psalm 25:10* "All the ways of the Lord are loving and faithful for those who keep the demands of His covenant." And unfailing love [חסד (khesed)] *Psalm 107:8* "Let them give thanks to the Lord for His unfailing love and His wonderful deeds for men,"

The refrain throughout *Psalm 136*, - His love [חסד (khesed)] "Give thanks to the Lord, for He is good. His love endures forever."

The Hebrew word Ahab (מיבהא) for love as a noun describes a variety of intensely close emotional bonds. So Abraham loved his son Isaac (*Genesis 22:2*), Isaac loved his son Esau (*Genesis 25:28*), and "Israel loved Joseph more than all his children" (*Genesis 37:3*). In a more romantic manner, Isaac loved his wife Rebekah (*Genesis 24:67*), and Jacob loved Rachel (*Genesis 29:18*), but Delilah manipulated Samson by challenging his love for her (*Judges 14:16*). We are all called to love the Lord, by expressing obedience to His commandments (*Deuteronomy 6:5*), and to "love thy neighbor as thyself" (*Leviticus 19:18*). Moreover, "he that gets wisdom loves his own soul" (*Proverbs 19:8*).

New Testament Love
There are four Greek words for "Love" in the New Testament.

Phileō (Φιλέω) is a companion love that speaks of friendship, affection, fondness, delight, personal attachment, or liking. It is a love that responds to kindness or appreciation. It involves giving as well as receiving; but when it is greatly strained, it can collapse in a crisis. This love is called out of one's heart by qualities in another. In *John 21:15-17*, it is contrasted with *agape* love. The word *phileo* is one of feeling – a heart of love – whereas *agape* is a matter of benevolence, duty, and commitment. You will find this kind of love in: *Matthew 6:5, 10:37, 23:6, 26:48; Mark 14:44; Luke 20:46, 22:47; John 5:20, 11:3, 36, 12:25, 15:19, 16:27, 20:2, 21:15, 21:16-17; 1 Corinthians 16:22; Titus 3:15;* and *Revelations 3:19, 22:15*.

Agapē or Agapaō (Ἀγάπη or Ἀγαπάω) is called out of one's heart by the preciousness of the object loved. It is a love of esteem, of evaluation. It has the idea of prizing. Like its synonym *philia*, it designates love between persons (*John 13:35*), or people for God (*1 John 2:15*), of God for humanity (*Romans 5:8*), and of God for Christ (*John 17:26*).

Whereas *phila* emphasizes the idea of love arising from personal relationships, *agape* is founded upon deep appreciation and high regard. It is perhaps for this reason that *agape* is the love which God commands. It is the noblest word for love in the Greek language. God's love is described as this Greek word *agapao*, which means unconditional love, preferential love that is chosen and acted out by the will.

It is not love based on the goodness of the beloved, or upon natural affinity or emotion. Rather this is benevolent love that always seeks the good of the beloved. This type of love is exclusive to Christians because it flows directly from God's love: "Beloved, let us love one another: for love is of God; and everyone that loves is born of God, and knows God. He that loves not knows not God; for God is love" (*1 John 4:7,8*).

Agapē is not kindled by the merit or worth of it's object, but it originates in it's own God-given nature. God is love. It delights in giving. This love keeps on loving even when the loved one is unresponsive, unkind, unlovable, and unworthy. It is unconditional love. *Agapē* desires only the good of the one loved. It is a consuming passion for the well-being of others.

There are only a few known occurrences of this word "love" outside of the Bible. In other words, this word was not used very often in extra-biblical writings. It is used approximately three hundred and twenty times in the New Testament. You will find this kind of love in: *John 3:16, 3:35, 13:34, 14:15, 15:9, 15:13; Romans 5:5, 13:8-10; Galatians 5:22; Ephesians 3:17, 4:2, 4:15, 5:2, 5:25; Colossians 3:14; 1 Thessalonians 3:12, 4:9-10;* and *1 Peter 4:8 3.*

Storgē (Στοργή) This love has its basis in one's own nature. It is a natural affection or natural obligation. It is a natural movement of the soul for husband, wife, child or dog. It is a quiet, abiding feeling within a man that rests on something close to him and that he feels good about.

In the New Testament *storgē* appears in the noun or verb form with the prefix "a" and therefore negates the love and means without this type of love. It is translated in *Romans 1:31* and *2 Timothy 3:3* as "unloving" (without natural affection). In *Romans 12:10, storgē* is compounded with *philos* and is translated "devoted" (kindly affectioned). You will find this kind of love in: *Romans 1:31, 12:10;* and *2 Timothy 3:3 4.*

Eros (Ερος) This love is erotic love. *Eros* is a love of passion, an overmastering passion that seizes and absorbs itself into the mind. It is a love that is an emotional involvement based on body chemistry. The basic idea of this love is self-satisfaction.

Though *Eros* is directed towards another, it actually has self in mind. For example: "I love you because you make me happy." The foundation of this type of love is some characteristic in the other person which pleases you. If the characteristic would cease to exist, the reason for the love would be gone, the result being, "I don't love you anymore."

Eros looks for what it can receive. If it does give, it gives in order to receive. If it fails to get what it wants or expects, bitterness or resentment could develop. The philosophy of *eros* is that being loved depends on being attractive in some way to another person. Because of this dependency, *eros* would be considered a conditional type of love. *Eros* is not used in the New Testament. *Eros* is not used in the Septuagint. (The Septuagint, abbreviated LXX, is the Greek translation of the Old Testament.) It is used a lot in Greek mythology.

Want Versus Need

God, I love you and I need you. A "want" is something you would like to have. It is not absolutely necessary, but it would be a good thing to have. A "want" is simply something that people desire to have, that they may, or may not, be able to obtain.

The idea of survival is real, meaning someone would die without their "needs" being met. This includes things like food, water, and shelter. You might not need a whole lot of food, but you do need to eat. Jesus declared, "I am the bread of life. Whoever comes to Me will never go hungry, and whoever believes in Me will never be thirsty." (*John 6:35*)

If you love God, you need to embrace Him in every hour of your day. Remember, God has fallen in love with you forever.

CHAPTER 15 - LISTEN

I KNOW THAT WHEN I CAN'T PRAY, YOU LISTEN TO MY HEART.

No matter how softly you whisper a prayer, God surely listens, understands and knows the hopes and fears you keep in your heart. And when you trust Him, miracles happen.

"But the Lord said to Samuel, "Do not consider his appearance or his height, for I have rejected him. The Lord does not look at the things man looks at. Man looks at the outward appearance, but the Lord looks at the heart." (1 Samuel 16:7)

Have A Heart

The end of December 2008 held a surprise for us. I had a mild heart attack (myocardial infarction) while helping a neighbor change a tire on the Monday night before Christmas. When finished, I returned home with severe chest pains, sweating, weak and dizzy. I looked up the symptoms on *"Google"* and it gave me the red flag 'heart attack'. I told my wife we were driving to the hospital. (Yes, I drove.)

In the E.R., an EKG was taken, 3 nitro tablets were administered and at least 15 gallons of blood were extracted – it sure felt like it. Blood tests were made that can measure the level of cardiac muscle enzymes and proteins called troponins. These proteins control the interactions that contract or squeeze the heart muscle. Troponins specific to heart muscles can detect heart muscle injury.

"You will seek me and find me when you seek me with all your heart." (Jeremiah 29:13)

They confirmed that I indeed had a mild heart attack with no permanent heart muscle damage. My wife remained with me in the hospital 24/7, sleeping in my room or in a waiting room while I was in ICU. After treatment of several I.V.'s, I was going to be released from the hospital on Wednesday morning. As a precaution, one of the cardiologists prescribed a heart medication called 'Lisinapril'. This caused my heart rate to drop below 30 and my blood pressure to 60/30 – then flat-lining. A major panic broke out in my room. Paddles attached, I.V.'s again installed, nitro tablets, blood tests, multiple injections of atropine - used in the treatment of bradycardia (an extremely low heart rate). Thank the Lord, with God's hands the doctors and nurses were able to revive me.

"But I, the Lord, search all hearts and examine secret motives. I give all people their due rewards, according to what their actions deserve." (Jeremiah 17:10)

I remained in the hospital through Friday evening, having a heart catheter procedure that showed that my arteries and valves had no blockages or damage. The initial impact was only to the heart muscles, which were already beginning to heal. Praise the Lord! We celebrated Christmas Eve and Christmas Day together in the hospital that year.

The doctors think that the heart attack was caused from a series of events –my COPD reduces the amount of oxygen provided to my heart and blood supply. When applying physical stress to loosen the lug nuts for removing the tire, I momentarily held my breath causing 0% oxygen supply, which ultimately caused the 100% shut-off of any blood supply to my heart. (No more changing tires for me.)

They put me on a different heart medication designed to increase my heart rate and relax the blood vessels so that the blood can flow more freely without putting additional strain on my heart.

Other than a side effect of being lightheaded, they said to just continue to watch my blood pressure. With God at my side (and most of the time carrying me), I feel great.

Take A Moment

Shortly after my heart attack, my employer reorganized. This was a stressful time for us since I was just recovering from the shock of the Christmas heart attack. Well, they completed the reorganization, and although 106 employees lost their jobs in my department, God saw fit to keep me employed. Thank you Lord. Praise be Your Name!

The minor heart attack and reorganization didn't shake my love for Jesus. His love only strengthens me. The warmth of the Holy Spirit comes into my heart every day and I rejoice in being alive for Him.

Today we seem to be in a constant hurry. We find ourselves so busy that we seldom stop, look and listen. But, God is always listening. "In the same way, the Spirit helps us in our weakness. We do not know what we ought to pray for, but the Spirit himself intercedes for us with groans that words cannot express. And He who searches our hearts knows the mind of the Spirit, because the Spirit intercedes for the saints in accordance with God's will." (*Romans 8:26-27*) All we have to do is take a moment to talk to Him.

Quality Of Life

I was a full-time employee working out of the home office for a financial company for almost 10 years in Phoenix, Arizona. I had set up the garage in several of our rental homes as my woodworking shop and had custom built an autoharp and a banjo for my daughter and son-in-law, along with other smaller projects. In March of 2014, we purchase a home. There is no garage, so I finally sold all of my woodworking equipment and purchased a golf cart with the proceeds so that I could drive to the club house to get the mail. I soon found that the air quality in Phoenix was such that I was not able to use an open vehicle.

My health still has its moments as the chronic obstructive pulmonary disease (COPD) continues to worsen; the cells in the airways continue to make more mucus causing the airways to clog more often. I was on oxygen overnight from 2009 until 2016 when Medicare requirements said I know longer needed it. (What?) My lung capacity is now at 27% so far, and will continue to be reduced by this lung disease. Every once in a while I get an occasional angina tap on my heart as a reminder of Who is in control of my life.

Stop. Look, Listen
I remember what they taught us in school regarding train tracks – "**Stop. Look, Listen**". As America became laced with railroads in the latter half of the 19th century, it became apparent that safety warning signs and signals should be set up to protect people who wanted to cross the tracks.

Initially, signs were posted at crossings, and watchmen were stationed at the busier crossings to warn of approaching trains. The first U.S. patent given for a railroad crossing gate was on August 27, 1867. At that time, crossing gates were hand-operated by means of a crank mechanism. The gates were lowered and raised by means of cables or chains running through underground piping from the gatekeeper's crank base to each individual gate at the crossing. As a train approached, the gatekeeper would crank the gates, and these would remain down until the train passed safely. By the early 20th century, the use of "crossbuck" signs (the boards forming an "X"), were very common. The design formed the warning sign still in use today.

The first automatic crossing signals were bells mounted on top of poles. The electric bell idea was quickly expanded to include a swinging round sign with a red light hanging from an arm on the signal pole to simulate a flagman waving a red lantern. The "Automatic Flagman" signals were dubbed "Wig-Wags".

Eventually the Wig-Wags gave way to the alternating flashing red lights mounted as part of a cross-buck sign, and often with the crossing gates as well. The first flashing red light signal was installed in New Jersey in 1913.

In addition to the signals and signs, operating rules require train crews to sound the locomotive horn or whistle a quarter of a mile in advance of each public crossing until they cross the roadway. Modern locomotives are equipped with a triangle of bright headlights, one mounted high and centered, and two on each lower side of the front of the engine. As soon as the horn begins to sound, the lower twin lights are illuminated and flash alternately. Physics makes it impossible to stop a moving train in time to avoid striking a motorist or pedestrian on the track. Signals, signs, lights, whistles and horns are important safety aids, but ultimately it is the motorist's responsibility to determine whether or not it is safe to cross the tracks. **Always remember to STOP, LOOK AND LISTEN!** God doesn't need automated warning signals to listen to our heart. He is always there, waiting for us.

Eyes Of Your Heart
Diana Ross sang a song called "Stop! Look, Listen (To Your Heart)":

> *Stop, look, yes, listen to your heart*
> *Hear what it's sayin'*
> *Stop, look, listen to your heart*
> *Hear what it's sayin'*
> *Love, oh, love, love.*

God sent His Holy Spirit to dwell in our hearts. Paul was very clear in his prayer to the Ephesians - "I pray also that the eyes of your heart may be enlightened in order that you may know the hope to which He has called you, the riches of His glorious inheritance in the saints." (*Ephesians 1:18*)

God loves us so much that He gave us His Son. "For God is greater than our hearts, and He knows everything." *(1 John 3:20)*

CHAPTER 16 - INVITE

COME INTO MY HEART, PLEASE!

Give Your Life To Christ

Somewhere between the 5th and 6th grade, I gave my life to Christ. I can't tell you exactly when, because I was talking with God or reading His Word almost daily. It seemed like such a natural thing to do. God was always with me every day. He had protected me during the car accident, was with me during the trials of my 'heart condition' and blessed me with Christian parents who cared enough to share the Lord in my life. (I will forever be grateful for their love and support.)

When I reached the sixth grade, God actually spoke to me. He told me that I should be a minister. (Now who is going to argue with God?) I shared this with my parents. At first, they were hesitant, but after several conversations, they finally believed me and understood my true desires to serve our Lord.

"Because you are sons, God sent the Spirit of his Son into our hearts, the Spirit who calls out, Abba, Father." (Galatians 4:6)

"Here I am! I stand at the door and knock. If anyone hears My voice and opens the door, I will come in and eat with him, and he with Me." (Revelations 3:20)

Witness

There is a mysterious relationship between people and the God who reveals Himself in the Bible as Creator, Redeemer and Lover/Beloved of each person who chooses to accept His invitation.

There is an overwhelming warm feeling in your heart when you can invite someone to your Lord and they accept that invitation. As a Youth League counselor at our church, we organized a witness event where the youth were assigned, 2 by 2, with an adult as we went out into the community. We shared our witness and the love of Jesus. Several were brought to Christ. We give God the glory for His grace.

"If you declare with your mouth, 'Jesus is Lord,' and believe in your heart that God raised Him from the dead, you will be saved. For it is with your heart that you believe and are justified, and it is with your mouth that you profess your faith and are saved." (*Romans 10:9-10*)

What a wonderful feeling when God calls us His children. It is so comforting to know that He makes His home within us so we can rest secure in Him. Because He is our dwelling place, we are never alone.

"For the eyes of the Lord range throughout the earth to strengthen those whose hearts are fully committed to Him. "
(2 Chronicles 16:9)

"The Word became flesh and made His dwelling among us. We have seen His glory, the glory of the One and Only, who came from the Father, full of grace and truth."
(John 1:14)

Anchor Your Trust In God

Jim Cymbala points out that we shouldn't focus on our troubles. Instead, we need to celebrate that God has already demonstrated His power and provision in our past. We need to anchor our hearts and minds in God's overwhelming track record.

The Bible says, "Come near to God and He will come near to you." (*James 4:8*) Not all Christians live the same distance from God. Even though we all belong to His family, some are closer to His dynamic strength than others. As we live a life full of praise and thanksgiving for past mercies, we experience God coming ever closer to us in the present.

"I pray that out of His glorious riches He may strengthen you with power through His Spirit in your inner being, so that Christ may dwell in your hearts through faith. And I pray that you, being rooted and established in love, may have power, together with all the saints, to grasp how wide and long and high and deep is the love of Christ, and to know this love that surpasses knowledge—that you may be filled to the measure of all the fullness of God."
(Ephesians 3:16-19)

CHAPTER 17 – HOLY SPIRIT

I ASK THAT THE HOLY SPIRIT FILL MY HEART WITH YOUR LOVE.

Spirits can take on many forms. The English word "spirit", from the Latin *spiritus* "breath", has many different meanings and connotations, most of them relating to a mind-body experience contrasted with the physical body. The notion of a person's spirit and soul often overlap, as both contrast with body and are believed to survive bodily death in some religions. A "spirit" can also have the sense of "ghost", i.e. a manifestation of the spirit of a deceased person.

Ghostly Example

When I was in the second grade, my grandfather would typically sit in his reserved rocking chair in the living room. We loved to bounce balloons back and forth with him, or have horsey rides on the end of his leg. During the time we lived in Brooklyn Center, my grandfather passed away. He had diabetes.

"Anyone who believes in the Son of God has this testimony in his heart. Anyone who does not believe God has made him out to be a liar, because he has not believed the testimony God has given about His Son." (1 John 5:10)

"In his heart a man plans his course, but the Lord determines his steps." (Proverbs 16:9)

My bedroom was right across from the main bathroom and each night after his death, I could still see him walking down the hallway in his nightshirt to the bathroom and then into the living room. He had a special rocking chair, and although I knew that he had died, I could still hear the rocker squeaking each night as it rocked back and forth.

Embracing Death

The Mississippi River was a great place to catch carp and turtles. My friend and I would often follow the shoreline for a few miles south to the highway bridge. While a Cub Scout, one of our scouts had built a raft and traveled the swift current of the Mississippi River. Unfortunately, as he was fishing from his raft, the tackle box fell into the water. He was a good swimmer and jumped in after it. The current was too much for him and he lost his life. Our entire troop was at the funeral. I never went back to the Mississippi River shoreline after that.

Sadness hit our family one October night. A large truck hit and killed my daughters' best friend, who was with child. This was devastating for our entire family. She and my daughter had been best friends since elementary school. Unfortunately, as time goes by, I have lost contact with most of my friends, either through distance or death.

"And you, my son Solomon, acknowledge the God of your father, and serve Him with wholehearted devotion and with a willing mind, for the Lord searches every heart and understands every motive behind the thoughts. If you seek Him, He will be found by you; but if you forsake Him, He will reject you forever."
(1 Chronicles 28:9)

"He saved us, not by the righteous deeds we had done, but according to His mercy, through the washing of new birth and renewal by the Holy Spirit."
(Titus 3:5)

Even in our marriage vows we see reference to death. "To have and to hold, from this day forward, for better or for worse, for richer or for poorer, in sickness and in health, to love and to cherish, till death us do part."

The following description of death was written by Henry Scott Holland (27 January 1847 – 17 March 1918) as Regius Professor of Divinity at the University of Oxford:

> *"Death is nothing at all. It does not count. I have only slipped away into the next room. Nothing has happened. Everything remains exactly as it was. I am I, and you are you, and the old life that we lived so fondly together is untouched, unchanged. Whatever we were to each other that we are still. Call me by the old familiar name. Speak of me in the easy way which you always used. Put no difference into your tone.*
>
> *Wear no forced air of solemnity or sorrow. Laugh as we always laughed at the little jokes that we enjoyed together. Play, smile, think of me, and pray for me. Let my name be ever the household word that it always was. Let it be spoken without an effort, without the ghost of a shadow upon it. Life means all that it ever meant. It is the same as it ever was. There is absolute and unbroken continuity. What is this death but a negligible accident? Why should I be out of mind because I am out of sight? I am but waiting for you, for an interval, somewhere very near, just round the corner. All is well."*

God tells us, "He will wipe away every tear from their eyes; and death shall be no more. Neither shall there be mourning, nor crying, nor pain anymore; for the former things have passed away." (*Revelation 21:4*)

Halloween Eve

Halloween, also known as All Hallows' Eve, or All Saints' Eve, is a celebration observed in a number of countries on October 31st, the eve of the Western Christian feast of All Hallows' Day. It begins the three-day observance of Allhallowtide, the time in the liturgical year dedicated to remembering the dead, including saints (hallows), martyrs, and all the faithful departed. It is widely believed that many Halloween traditions originated from Celtic harvest festivals which may have pagan roots, particularly the Gaelic festival Samhain, and that this festival was Christianized as Halloween.

Halloween activities include trick-or-treating, attending Halloween costume parties, carving pumpkins into jack-o'-lanterns, lighting bonfires, apple bobbing, playing pranks, visiting haunted attractions, telling scary stories and watching horror films. In many parts of the world, the Christian religious observances of All Hallows' Eve, including attending church services and lighting candles on the graves of the dead, remain popular.

All Saints' Day

All Saints' Day is a celebration of all Christian saints. In Western Christianity, it is celebrated on November 1st by the Roman Catholic Church, the Anglican Communion, the Methodist, Lutheran, and other Protestant churches. The Eastern Orthodox Church and associated Eastern Catholic churches celebrate it on the first Sunday after Pentecost. Oriental Orthodox churches of Chaldea and associated Eastern Catholic churches celebrate All Saints' Day on the first Friday after Easter. Many Christians visit the graves of their loved ones, where they light candles and leave flowers.

Pope Gregory IV made All Saints' Day an authorized holiday in 837 CE. It is speculated that the chosen date for the event, November 1, may have been an attempt to replace the pagan Festival of the Dead (known as Samhain or the feast of Saman, lord of death). Other sources say that a commemoration of "All Martyrs" began as early as 270 CE but no specific month or date is recorded.

Note: The older terminology for dividing time was AD and BC, the one meaning anno domini (in the year of our Lord) and the other meaning "before Christ." All time in the western world has been looked at through this lens. It is a distinctively Christian view of things. In the last few years, some Christian scholars (and several non-Christian writers) have begun to use CE and BCE, which refer to the "Common Era" and "Before the Common Era" respectively. Such a perspective is not necessarily hostile to the Christian faith. Rather, it simply does not affirm the explicitly Christian demarcations for time.

Christian celebration of All Saints' Day and All Souls' Day stems from a belief that there is a powerful spiritual bond between those in heaven (the "Church triumphant"), and the living (the "Church militant"). In Catholic theology, the day commemorates all those who have attained the joyful vision in Heaven. It is a national holiday in many historically Catholic countries.

In Methodist theology, All Saints Day revolves around "giving God thanks for the lives and deaths of his saints", including those who are "famous ". Individuals throughout the Church Universal are honored, such as Paul the Apostle, Augustine of Hippo, Martin Luther and John Wesley. In addition, those who have personally led one to faith in Jesus, such as one's grandmother or friend.

In the British Isles, churches celebrate All Saints on November 1st to coincide or replace the Celtic festival of Samhain. In France, the day is known as La Toussaint. Flowers (especially Chrysanthemums), or wreaths called 'couronnes de toussaints' are placed at each tomb or grave. The following day, November 2nd (All Souls' Day) is called Le jour des morts, the Day of the Dead.

In Mexico, Guatemala, Portugal and Spain, offerings are made on this day. All Saints' Day in Mexico, coincides with the first day of the Day of the Dead (Spanish: Día de los Muertos) celebration. Known as "Día de los Inocentes" (Day of the Innocents), it honors deceased children and infants. Day of the Dead is a Mexican holiday celebrated throughout Mexico, in particular the Central and South regions, and by people of Mexican ancestry living in other places, especially the United States. It is acknowledged internationally in many other cultures. The multi-day holiday focuses on gatherings of family and friends to pray for and remember friends and family members who have died, and help support their spiritual journey.

Portuguese children celebrate the Pão-por-Deus tradition (also called santorinho, bolinho or fiéis de Deus) going door-to-door, where they receive cakes, nuts, pomegranates, sweets and candies. Hallow-mas in the Philippines is variously called "Undás", "Todos los Santos" (Spanish, "All Saints"), and sometimes "Araw ng mga Patay / Yumao" (Tagalog, "Day of the dead / those who have passed away"). Filipinos traditionally observe this day by visiting the family dead to clean and repair their tombs. Offerings of prayers, flowers, candles, and even food are made, while Chinese Filipinos additionally burn incense and kim. Many also spend the day and ensuing night holding reunions at the graves, playing games and music, singing karaoke, and feasting.

In Argentina, Austria, Belgium, Bolivia, Chile, France, Hungary, Italy, Lebanon, Luxembourg, Malta, Peru, Portugal, Puerto Rico, and Spain, people take flowers to the graves of dead relatives. In Austria, Bosnia and Herzegovina, Croatia, the Czech Republic, Finland, Catholic parts of Germany, Hungary, Italy, Lithuania, Macedonia, Moldova, Poland, Romania, Slovakia, Slovenia, Serbia and Sweden, the tradition is to light candles and visit the graves of deceased relatives.

In English-speaking countries, the festival is traditionally celebrated with the hymn "For All the Saints" by Walsham How. The most familiar tune for this hymn is Sine Nomine by Ralph Vaughan Williams.

Demons and Exorcism

The term "spirit" may also refer to demons or deities. There are at least sixty references to demons in the Bible. "They sacrificed to demons, not God, to gods they had not known, new gods that had just arrived, which your fathers did not fear." (*Deuteronomy 32:17*) In the four Gospels, we find at least twenty-five versus where Jesus cast out demons. For example "When evening came, they brought to Him many who were demon-possessed; and He

cast out the spirits with a word, and healed all who were ill. "
(*Matthew 8:16*)

Exorcism (from Greek ἐξορκισμός, exorkismos – binding by oath) is the religious practice of evicting demons from a person or an area they are believed to have possessed. Depending on the spiritual beliefs of the exorcist, this may be done by causing the entity to swear an oath, performing an elaborate ritual, or simply by commanding it to depart in the name of a higher power. The practice is ancient and part of the belief system of many cultures.

In Christian practice the person performing the exorcism, known as an exorcist, is often a member of the Christian Church, or an individual thought to be graced with special powers or skills. The exorcist often invokes God, Jesus and/or several different angels and archangels to intervene with the exorcism. Christian exorcists most commonly believe the authority given to them is through the Holy Trinity and the source of their ability to cast out demons.

In Catholic Christianity, exorcisms are performed in the name of Jesus Christ. A distinction is made between a formal exorcism, which can only be conducted by a priest during a baptism or with the permission of a Bishop, and "prayers of deliverance" which can be said by anyone. Priests are instructed to carefully determine that the nature of the affliction is not actually a psychological or physical illness before proceeding.

Beliefs and practices pertaining to the practice of exorcism are prominently connected with Hindus. Of the four Vedas (holy books of the Hindus), the Atharva Veda is said to contain the secrets related to exorcism, magic and alchemy. The basic means of exorcism are the mantra and the yajna used in both Vedic and Tantric traditions. Vaishnava traditions also employ a recitation of names of Narasimha and reading scriptures aloud. Kirtan, continuous playing of mantras, keeping scriptures and holy pictures of the deities (Shiva, Vishnu, Hanuman, Brahma, Shakti.) (especially of Narasimha) in the house, burning incense offered during a Puja, sprinkling water from holy rivers, and blowing conches used in puja are other effective practices. It is also believed that, praying to Lord Hanuman, gives the best result. It is also mentioned in the Hanuman Chalisa. It is believed that just uttering the name of Lord Hanuman makes the evil forces and devils tremble, in fear.

In Islam, exorcism is called ruqya. It is used to repair the damage caused by sihr or black magic. Exorcisms today are part of a wider body of contemporary Islamic alternative medicine called al-Tibb al-Nabawi (Medicine of the Prophet). Islamic exorcisms consist of the treated person lying down, while a sheikh places a hand on a patient's head while reciting verses from the Quran. The drinking or sprinkling of holy water (water from the Zamzam Well) may also take place along with applying of clean non-alcohol-based perfumes, called as ittar. Specific verses from the Quran are recited, which glorify God (e.g. The Throne Verse (Arabic: آية الكرسي Ayatul Kursi)), and invoke God's help. In some cases, the adhan (call for daily prayers) is also read, as this has the effect of repelling non-angelic unseen beings or the jinn. The Islamic prophet Muhammad taught his followers to read the last three suras from the Quran, Surat al-Ikhlas (The Fidelity), Surat al-Falaq (The Dawn) and Surat an-Nas (Mankind).

Today, the procedure for a Jewish exorcism is intended not only to drive away the possessing force, but to help both the possessor and the possessed in healing. The Jewish exorcism ritual is performed by a rabbi who has mastered practical Kabbalah. Also present is a minyan (a group of ten adult males), who gather in a circle around the possessed person. The group recites *Psalm 91* three times, and then the rabbi blows a shofar (a ram's horn). The shofar is blown with various notes, in effect to "shatter the body" so that the possessing force will be shaken loose. After it has been shaken loose, the rabbi begins to communicate with it and ask it questions such as why it is possessing the body of the possessed. The minyan may pray and perform a ceremony in order to enable it to feel safe, and leave the person's body.

Purgatory

Purgatory is an often-misunderstood Catholic doctrine. Roman Catholics believe in Heaven, Hell, and something called Purgatory that has two purposes: a temporal punishment for sin, and the cleansing from the attachment to sin. Purgatory purifies the soul before the soul's grand entrance into heaven. In Catholic theology, Purgatory (Latin: Purgatorium, via Anglo-Norman and Old French) is an intermediate state after physical death in which those destined for heaven "undergo purification, so as to achieve the holiness necessary to enter the joy of heaven".

Belief in Purgatory is not present in Islam. Many consider grave (Al-Barzakh) as Purgatory. But there is no similarity of it with Christian Purgatory. When a Muslim person dies, he is asked three questions in the grave by two angels, Munkar and Nakir.

Holy Spirit

In the Bible, "the Spirit" (with a capital "S"), specifically denotes the Holy Spirit. *Matthew 12:32* says, "And whoever speaks a word against the Son of Man will be forgiven; but whoever speaks against the holy Spirit will not be forgiven, either in this age or in the age to come." Here Jesus speaks of sin against the Holy Spirit. The implication is that some sins can be forgiven in the world to come.

We know that in Hell there is no liberation and in Heaven nothing imperfect can enter it. Sin is not forgiven when a soul reaches its final destination because in heaven there is no need for forgiveness of sin and in hell the choice to go there is already made.

"Not only so, but we also rejoice in our sufferings, because we know that suffering produces perseverance; perseverance, character; and character, hope. And hope does not disappoint us, because God has poured out his love into our hearts by the Holy Spirit, whom he has given us." (*Romans 5:3-5*)

Pentecost

"Go ye therefore, and teach all nations, baptizing them in the name of the Father, and of the Son, and of the Holy Ghost. Teaching them to observe all things whatsoever I have commanded you: and, lo, I am with you always, even unto the end of the world. Amen." (*Matthew 28:19-20*)

Pentecost is the Christian festival celebrating the descent of the Holy Spirit on the disciples of Jesus after His Ascension, held on the seventh Sunday after Easter and the Jewish festival of Shavuot. In the New Testament (*Acts 2:1-13*), the day that the Holy Spirit descended upon the disciples of Jesus. Pentecost is the Greek name for Shavuot, the spring harvest festival of the Israelites, which was going on when the Holy Spirit came.

When the Holy Spirit came upon the apostles and the other believers on the Day of Pentecost, those who heard those speaking in tongues were perplexed and asked, "What does this mean?" (*Acts 2:12*) Many claim that the meaning of Pentecost is that we should have the same experience as the disciples, namely, that we are to seek the baptism of the Holy Spirit.

Acts 2 must be interpreted in light of *Acts 1:4-8*, where the risen Lord Jesus instructed the disciples to wait in Jerusalem for the promise of the Father, the Holy Spirit. Jesus explained that they would "be baptized with the Holy Spirit not many days from now" (*Acts 1:5*) and they would receive power to be Christ's "witnesses both in Jerusalem, and in all Judea and Samaria, and even to the remotest part of the earth" (*Acts 1:8*). Just as the ministry of Jesus depended on the Holy Spirit descending on Him at His baptism, so the ministry of the disciples depended on them receiving the Holy Spirit and relying on His power. While they had experienced a measure of the Spirit's power before (*John 20:22*), now He would come to dwell in them permanently (*John 7:37-39; 14:17*).

Acts 2 was a special historical event, signifying a new period in God's dealings with His people. Pentecost signals the dawning of the age of the Holy Spirit. And the fullness of the Spirit in God's people is to empower them for witness to all the nations. Thus, the meaning of Pentecost is God's equipping His church with the power of His Spirit so that He will be glorified among the nations.

To understand this event, we must understand the Jewish Feast of Pentecost. It was not by coincidence that God poured out His Spirit on the disciples on that day. There were three great Jewish feasts each year: Passover (in the spring), celebrating Israel's deliverance from Egypt, followed immediately by the Feast of Unleavened Bread; Pentecost, also called the Feast of Weeks, which occurred 50 days (seven weeks) after Passover; and, Tabernacles (in the fall). Pentecost was an initial harvest feast, where the Jews were to offer to the Lord the first fruits of the new grain. They were to wave before the Lord two loaves of wheat bread, made with leaven (*Leviticus 23:15-21*).

This picture came to fulfillment in the outpouring of the Holy Spirit on the Day of Pentecost. Until this time, the Lord's people consisted of Israel, along with a few Gentile proselytes. Not all in Israel were believers, but it was through that nation exclusively that God worked through His covenant promises to form a people for Himself.

But now the Lord formed the body of Christ, the church, made up of Jews and Gentiles on equal footing. Paul calls this inclusion of the Gentiles in the church a mystery, meaning that it had not been formerly revealed (*Ephesians 3:4-7*), although it was typified in this Jewish feast with two loaves. That these two loaves were made up of leavened bread pictures the fact that although we are redeemed in Christ, we are still sinners who must learn to get along with those who, in the flesh, are very different than we are.

You may recall that the Lord had told Peter that He would build His church and the gates of hell would not prevail against it (*Matthew 16:18*). Thus the church, founded on the apostolic confession and witness of Christ, is God's means of taking the gospel to the nations, resulting in His being glorified in all the earth. "God did not call us to be impure, but to live a holy life. Therefore, anyone who rejects this instruction does not reject a human being but God, the very God who gives you his Holy Spirit" (*1 Thessalonians 4:7-8*).

The Instruction Manual

The B.I.B.L.E. can be expanded to mean "Basic Information Before Leaving Earth". The Bible is our instruction manual about life. I have not discovered anything in my life that has not already been told in the Bible, including what to do about it.

There is no holy living outside of the Holy Spirit's control. If the Holy Spirit is forgotten in our spiritual walk, we fail to become the pure and joyful person that God has planned for us. We simply won't succeed.

The Holy Spirit works deep inside of us to change our desires from pleasing ourselves to pleasing God. He also uses the Word of God to enable us to control our thoughts in our lives. The Holy Spirit is the only one who can subdue the strong urgings of our human nature. He is the only one who can break habits that have been repeated countless times.

He is the only one who can overcome Satan and all his daily temptations. "Do you not know that your body is a temple of the Holy Spirit, who is in you, whom you have received from God? You are not your own; you were bought at a price. Therefore honor God with your body." (*1 Corinthians 6:19-20*)

CHAPTER 18 - EMBRACE

FATHER, I WANT TO EMBRACE YOU WITH MY ARMS AND FEEL THE WARMTH OF YOUR STRONG AND LOVING ARMS AROUND ME.

Lessons From My Parents

Mom loved to paint and wallpaper. Although I was young, on occasion I would help with the wallpaper. One wall of our dining room received many coats of paint and wallpaper through the years. If she didn't like the color or print, she would scrape it off and start over. I remember when the gallon of paint flipped off the ladder onto the tarp below. I also remember scraping the wallpaper off the wall twice in the same day. I love and miss my mom who went to heaven on my 51st birthday.

I can also remember the big March 22, 1952 winter blizzard that dumped more than 12 inches of fresh white snow on the Twin Cities. My parents and grandparents said that this wasn't as bad as the Armistice Day blizzard of November 11, 1940, but it still took my dad two days to shovel us out.

On one winter occasion in the 2nd grade, my dad offered to drive me to school. We had quite the snowstorm the night before. His hard work of building the limestone retaining wall next to our long set of steps to the front door were holding just fine with all of the snow drifts. He had a small telephone company coupe that was fully covered with snow. It only had one seat, so I would sit on an aluminum milk box behind the drivers' seat. He knew that this little car was raised higher than others in the neighborhood so he didn't bother to brush off the snow, nor shovel a path down the driveway. Instead, I remember him opening his driver-side door, looking out and putting it in reverse. Within a few seconds, he had plowed enough snow into his lap to cover his feet. I didn't go to school that day.

"No one has ever seen God, but God the One and Only, Who is at the Father's side, has made Him known." (John 1:18)

I remember the day my dad wanted to catch a gopher that had been tormenting our yard. I was about 10 years old at the time. We had a culvert at the end of our driveway to allow the rain to pass along the ditch in front of our house. My dad saw a gopher run into this culvert. He went to get the can of gasoline for the lawn mower, and a pitchfork, from the garage. He instructed me as follows: "I am going to set a fire at one end of the culvert, and when the gopher runs out, jab him with the pitchfork." He lit the gasoline, and before I could even think about dropping the pitchfork, that gopher was already 2 blocks down the road.

"From the ends of the earth I call to You, I call as my heart grows faint; lead me to the rock that is higher than I. For You have been my refuge, a strong tower against the foe. I long to dwell in Your tent forever and take refuge in the shelter of Your wings." (Psalm 61:2-4)

I remember dad building scaffolding so that he could paint the siding on the back of our house. He leaned the ladder against the scaffolding and told me to hold the ladder as he climbed up with the paint bucket. (I was about 11 years old at the time.) As he neared the top of the scaffolding, it began to tip over. I watched as the slow-motion decent of dad, ladder and paint were succumbed to gravity with the green paint creating an artistic arc design on the freshly painted redwood siding. (I didn't mention that he was very frugal with his nails. The scaffolding had been built with only one nail per cross-member with a slight shape of an ice cream cone, narrow on the bottom and wider at the top.)

Dad would typically lock up his tools. His excuse was that he did not want them to disappear. He also had several old boards in the garage from the scaffolding. There was a stairway leading from the garage to the basement making useable garage floor space more limited. Since he worked long hours, I had plenty of time in the summer to be creative, so I decided to repurpose his scaffolding wood. I built a platform over the stairway and stored the lawnmower and bikes above that stairway, being careful to return all tools to their rightful place in his "locked" toolbox. After discovering this new platform, he completed a close examination to ensure that it was sturdy and safe. My father went to heaven in 2001.

I must have inherited some of dad's traits because I was also protective of my tools as a father. Perhaps because my sons would use them in later years and these tools could be found in the backyard on occasion.

Loving Arms
Do you remember the warm feeling you get when your mom or dad gives you a big hug? It made me feel secure, protected and loved. Or, perhaps you enjoy the embrace of your spouse, or hugging your children and grandchildren. I really want to give God a great big bear hug!

What A Friend We Have In Jesus

There is an old hymn that I learned as a child in Sunday School called *"What a Friend We Have In Jesus"*. It is at the end of verse 3 that we find "In his arms he'll take and shield thee; thou wilt find a solace there."

What a Friend We Have In Jesus

1.	*What a friend we have in Jesus,*
all our sins and griefs to bear!
What a privilege to carry
everything to God in prayer!
O what peace we often forfeit,
O what needless pain we bear,
all because we do not carry
everything to God in prayer.

2.	*Have we trials and temptations?*
Is there trouble anywhere?
We should never be discouraged;
take it to the Lord in prayer.
Can we find a friend so faithful
who will all our sorrows share?
Jesus knows our every weakness;
take it to the Lord in prayer.

3.	*Are we weak and heavy laden,*
cumbered with a load of care?
Precious Savior, still our refuge;
take it to the Lord in prayer.
Do thy friends despise, forsake thee?
Take it to the Lord in prayer!
In his arms he'll take and shield thee;
thou wilt find a solace there.

PART 4

YOUR WILL

CHAPTER 19 – USE ME

CONTINUE TO USE ME TO DO YOUR WILL.

The will of God will never take you where the Grace of God will not protect you. When God takes something from your grasp, He's not punishing you, but merely opening your hands to receive something better. To get something you never had, you have to do something you never did.

"We are God's workmanship, created in Christ Jesus to do good works, which God prepared in advance for us to do." (Ephesians 2: 10)

The Tabernacle

In *Exodus 31* we read that God ordered a lot of work to be done on the tabernacle and the materials the people were to provide. "Then the Lord said to Moses, 'See, I have chosen Bezalel son of Uri, the son of Hur, of the tribe of Judah, and I have filled him with the Spirit of God, with wisdom, with understanding, with knowledge and with all kinds of skills— to make artistic designs for work in gold, silver and bronze, to cut and set stones, to work in wood, and to engage in all kinds of crafts. Moreover, I have appointed Oholiab son of Ahisamak, of the tribe of Dan, to help him.

"I cried out to God for help; I cried out to God to hear me. When I was in distress, I sought the Lord; at night I stretched out untiring hands and my soul refused to be comforted." (Psalm 77:1-2)

Also I have given ability to all the skilled workers to make everything I have commanded you:" (*Exodus 31:1-6*)

Moses knew the learning of the Egyptians, and, he was well acquainted with the words of God, and the visions of the Almighty; but he did not know how to engrave or embroider. There may have been some very talented men among the Israelites; but, having lived in bondage in Egypt, they probably weren't taught these arts either. They knew how to make brick and work with clay, but they probably were never brought up to work with gold or cut diamonds.

God dispenses His gifts, one gift to one, another to another, and all for the good of the whole body, both of mankind and of the church. When Christ sent his apostles to build the gospel tabernacle, two by two, he poured out His Spirit on them, to enable them to speak with tongues the wonderful works of God; not to work with metal, but to work on men. When God has work to do, He will give us the skills and talents to get the job done.

"If anyone chooses to do God's will, he will find out whether my teaching comes from God or whether I speak on my own."
(John 7:17)

"This is the confidence we have in approaching God: that if we ask anything according to His will, He hears us. And if we know that He hears us—whatever we ask—we know that we have what we asked of Him."
(1 John 5:14-15)

Opportunities

The Jaycees offered a lot of opportunity for leadership and creative projects. We sold trash bags, acquired and installed an oxygen aerator machine at the local Crystal Lake, and even tried to start a local newspaper with advertising. I held multiple positions, including Treasurer, Secretary, Chapter President and Northwest Regional Vice President. My wife even held the presidency of the women's' Jaycee chapter for a year. We went to a few regional conventions while her brother watched our children. At age 35 you no longer can be in the Jaycees – you are then referred to as an "exhausted rooster".

God asked me to share my family values, skills and faith to do His will in Sunday School teaching, Church choir, Easter plays, Christmas pageants, outdoor summertime musicals, youth counseling, Cub Scout Master, Boy Scout Leader, Jaycees, coaching soccer, baseball and track, family guitar sing-alongs and camping. He gave me these skills as gifts to share His wonderful love for us.

"May the God of peace, Who through the blood of the eternal covenant brought back from the dead our Lord Jesus, that great Shepherd of the sheep, equip you with everything good for doing His will, and may He work in us what is pleasing to Him, through Jesus Christ, to whom be glory for ever and ever. Amen."
(Hebrews 13:20-21)

"The Lord will fulfill His purpose for me; Your love, O Lord, endures forever— do not abandon the works of Your hands."
(Psalm 138:8)

His Will

The Holy Spirit equips ordinary men and women to do extraordinary things. The Holy Spirit uses us to do God's will and He directs individuals into kingdom work. (You can read *Acts 13:2-5* and find out how the Holy Spirit sent Barnabas and Saul to Cyprus.). If we don't believe this, we become insensitive to the voice of the Spirit, and we will miss wonderful things that God has planned for us. We will never experience the power of God in our lives and circumstances.

One moment in history is the greatest example of loving God. It took place on the night before Jesus died, as He talked to His Father in the garden of Gethsemane. Knowing that the next day He would face the physical, emotional, and spiritual torture of the cross, Jesus prayed, "Not my will, but Yours be done" (*Luke 22:42*). Jesus set aside anything He may have desired and determined to do only what the Father directed.

"It is better to take refuge in the Lord than to trust in man." (Psalm 118:8)

"Give praise to the Lord, proclaim His name; make known among the nations what He has done." (1 Chronicles 16:8))

"I am the vine, you are the branches. He who abides in Me, and I in him, bears much fruit; for without Me you can do nothing." (John 15:5

The Way

How do you prepare your mind to make such a decision to set aside everything to follow God's direction? Jesus shows the way. You set your direction by talking to God. The power to follow Jesus' example is found in being able to pray the prayer that Jesus prayed: "Not my will, Lord, but Yours be done."

The word 'sin' has lost its true meaning in our culture. Foods are labeled as "sinfully delicious." Sin is sexy, exciting, fun, and thrilling, and perceived as "something fun and enjoyable that God doesn't want me to do." Sin may also be hate, stealing, killings, and destroying.

Sin is choosing my will, despite what God says about His will. When I don't trust that His way will give me a life that satisfies my desires, I choose my will and ways — that's sin. To some people, it feels like no big deal because it's the way of the world. To God it feels like adultery.

CHAPTER 20 – BLESS ME

CONTINUE TO BLESS ME THAT I MAY BE A BLESSING TO OTHERS.

Worship

The tradition of a blessing or benediction has been a part of Jewish and Christian worship for generations. We can trace it back to the book of Numbers where Aaron and his sons bless the Israelites with this blessing. "The Lord bless you and keep you; the Lord make His face shine on you and be gracious to you; the Lord turn His face toward you and give you peace." (*Numbers 6:24-26*)

This is the oldest known Biblical text that has been found; amulets with these verses written on them have been found in graves dating from the First Temple Period.

"Who is wise and understanding among you? Let him show it by his good life, by deeds done in the humility that comes from wisdom."
(James 3:13)

"So those who have faith are blessed along with Abraham, the man of faith."
(Galatians 3:9)

A church service needs to have a definite conclusion. Many New Testament letters end with some form of praise to God and commendation of believers to the care and guidance of God. These and other forms of blessing can provide a satisfying indication that the gathering has ended, even though the fellowship and ministry of believers continues informally in various ways.

God's Breath

T. Scott Daniels once wrote about a friend that helped him think of the gathering for worship and the sending into the world as the inhaling and exhaling of God. When the people of God are called to worship, it is as though the Almighty breathes in and draws His people close to His heart. There we are loved. There we are heard. There we are spoken to. But then God exhales and by the breath of His Spirit sends His people into the world as salt and light. The call of the church is not to make the world a better place to live. The call is to become a community faithfully witnessing to and extending by faith the kind of life made possible only through the death and resurrection of God's Son.

"The Lord bless you and keep you; the Lord make His face shine on you and be gracious to you; the Lord turn His face toward you and give you peace."
(Numbers 6:24-26)

"You are the light of the world. A city on a hill cannot be hidden. Neither do people light a lamp and put it under a bowl. Instead they put it on its stand, and it gives light to everyone in the house. In the same way, let your light shine before men, that they may see your good deeds and praise your Father in heaven."
(Matthew 5:14-16)

When we pray in faith and ask God to work in our lives, our asking opens the door for His great work in our lives. But, we have to ask.

Jabez prayed a bold prayer to God in *1 Chronicles 4:10*. Despite his upbringing and surroundings, he dared to ask God for His blessing. "Oh, that You would bless me indeed." Are you asking for blessings, or are you letting your circumstances keep you from praying? Don't let a lack of asking keep you from God's best in your life. Let this inspire you to ask for God's blessing so you can walk in the fullness that God has for you and become everything God has created you to be.

CHAPTER 21 – STRENGTHEN ME

KEEP ME STRONG THAT I MAY HELP THE WEAK. KEEP ME UPLIFTED THAT I MAY HAVE WORDS OF ENCOURAGEMENT FOR OTHERS.

As a young child, I enjoyed going to Sunday school and Church every week. My mother was in the choir. Dressed in a choir robe, she would proceed from the front of the Church sanctuary, up the main aisle of the nave, continue through the narthex, up the winding steps toward the steeple bell tower, and sing from the balcony next to the organ. The massive pipe organ would resonate to the hymns as I stared at the ornate blue stain glass windows behind the altar and along each side of the nave. My dad was an usher, so my sisters and I would sit with my grandparents or aunt and uncle.

Sanctuary

We were taught that church was a place to worship God and show reverence by keeping quiet and sitting still. I respected and admired Pastor Stahlke as my mentor. He would stand high in the pulpit each Sunday in his black robe, as if he were close enough to touch heaven, and preach the Gospel of our Lord Jesus Christ. I was so intent and focused on hearing and concentrating on each word that, on a few occasions, I would faint when I stood up at the end of the sermon. My parents were concerned and brought me to a medical specialist.

The doctors determined that I had a heart condition called WPW syndrome (Wolff-Parkinson-White syndrome), a condition caused by an abnormality in the electrical system of the heart which normally tells the heart muscle when to contract. In later years, this condition disappeared. I also have a right bundle branch block in the heart muscle and a heart murmur from birth.

"The stone the builders rejected has become the capstone; the Lord has done this, and it is marvelous in our eyes." (Psalm 118:22-23)

Persevere

Paul wrote, "I can do everything through Him who gives me strength." (*Philippians 4:13*) He also wrote, "Do not throw away your confidence; it will be richly rewarded. You need to persevere so that when you have done the will of God, you will receive what He has promised." (*Hebrews 10:35-36*)

"So then, just as you received Christ Jesus as Lord, continue to live in Him, rooted and built up in Him, strengthened in the faith as you were taught, and overflowing with thankfulness." (Colossians 2:6-7)

Rewards

When the Apostle Paul made reference to "richly rewarded", he wasn't referring to money. Things money can't buy include:

Manners	Morals
Respect	Character
Common sense	Trust
Patience	

Have confidence in sharing this list of values to help the weak, while encouraging our brothers and sisters, as we move forward in witnessing the love of Jesus Christ with others.

Pass The Salt

John Ortberg once said that your mission is not about you. Jesus said, "You are the salt of the earth." (*Matthew 5:13*) But salt does not exist for itself. When is the last time you went to someone's home for a meal and said, "Man, this is great salt. Honey, how come we don't have salt like this at home? We gotta switch brands." Salt's calling is to lose itself in something much bigger and more glorious; and then it fulfills its destiny. We were made to count. We were made to be salt. But the quest for significance is a delicate dance. If I do it by myself for myself, it's death. If I do it with God for others, it's life.

Uplifted

We are uplifted by the words that the Apostle Paul wrote to the church of Thessalonia, "Therefore encourage one another and build each other up, just as in fact you are doing." (*1 Thessalonians 5:11*) The Holy Spirit will provide the words necessary for us to share God's love. In *Ephesians* we read, "Do not let any unwholesome talk come out of your mouths, but only what is helpful for building others up according to their needs, that it may benefit those who listen." (*Ephesians 4:29*)

"And have you completely forgotten this word of encouragement that addresses you as a father addresses his son? It says, 'My son, do not make light of the Lord's discipline, and do not lose heart when he rebukes you, because the Lord disciplines the one he loves, and He chastens everyone He accepts as His son. 'Endure hardship as discipline; God is treating you as His children. For what children are not disciplined by their father?" (Hebrews 12:5-7)

It is our privilege and desire to see people accept Jesus as their personal Savior. "We have different gifts, according to the grace given us. If a man's gift is prophesying, let him use it in proportion to his faith. If it is serving, let him serve; if it is teaching, let him teach; if it is encouraging, let him encourage; if it is contributing to the needs of others, let him give generously; if it is leadership, let him govern diligently; if it is showing mercy, let him do it cheerfully." (*Romans 12:6-8*) The experience of sharing Jesus in and of itself is uplifting and rewarding.

By staying uplifted through renewed strength provided by the Holy Spirit, we have hope and can help the weak in spirit and encourage them to follow Jesus. "Do you not know? Have you not heard? The Lord is the everlasting God, the Creator of the ends of the earth. He will not grow tired or weary, and His understanding no one can fathom. He gives strength to the weary and increases the power of the weak. Even youths grow tired and weary, and young men stumble and fall; but those who hope in the Lord will renew their strength. They will soar on wings like eagles, they will run and not grow weary, they will walk and not be faint." (*Isaiah 40:28-31*) As David once said, "God is our refuge and strength, an ever-present help in trouble." (*Psalm 46:1*)

CHAPTER 22 – OPPORTUNITIES

REMIND ME TO SAY "THANK YOU", "I LOVE YOU" AND "I'M SORRY" AS EACH OPPORTUNITY ARISES.

Be Polite

I was raised to be polite, have manners and to respect my elders. This way of behaving toward people and the ways that are socially correct show respect for others included saying "Thank You". I pray that our society continues to instill manners into all children, rather than seen as entitlement by many?

"A man finds joy in giving an apt reply— and how good is a timely word!" (Proverbs 15:23)

Apologies

Many years ago I said something or did something that caused my relatives to quit talking to me. To this day I have no clue what the issue really was. However, I did write a formal apology that I entitled "Apologia". The origin of apologia is from the Latin and from Greek: a speaking in defense. Rather than blaming or pointing fingers in an attempt at always being right, it never hurts to humble yourself and just say "I'm sorry".

"You are my God, and I will give You thanks; You are my God, and I will exalt You. Give thanks to the Lord, for He is good; His love endures forever." (Psalm 118: 28-29)

Tame Your Tongue

Learn to tame your tongue for the glory of God our Father. *Titus 3:2* says "To speak evil of no one, to avoid quarreling, to be gentle, and to show perfect courtesy toward all people." And in *Proverbs 21:23* "Whoever keeps his mouth and his tongue keeps himself out of trouble."

The tongue, as a muscle, may not be as strong as the glutes, jaw or heart but strengthening it may still be useful. The tongue can stain the whole body, setting on fire the entire course of life, and set on fire by hell. Every kind of beast and bird, of reptile and sea creature, can be tamed and has been tamed by mankind, but no human being can tame the tongue. It is a restless evil, full of deadly poison. *Psalm 19:14* explains "Let the words of my mouth and the meditation of my heart be acceptable in your sight, O Lord, my rock and my redeemer."

Appreciation

In *Luke 17:11-19* we see that Jesus healed ten men with leprosy. This story reminds us to say "thank you" as each opportunity arises.

"I do not cease to give thanks for you, remembering you in my prayers."
(Ephesians 1:16)

"I thank my God in all my remembrance of you."
(Philippians 1:33)

"We always thank God, the Father of our Lord Jesus Christ, when we pray for you."
(Colossians 1:3)
"May the Lord reward you for your kindness."
(Ruth 1:8)

"Now on His way to Jerusalem, Jesus traveled along the border between Samaria and Galilee. As He was going into a village, ten men who had leprosy met Him. They stood at a distance and called out in a loud voice, "Jesus, Master, have pity on us!" When He saw them, He said, "Go, show yourselves to the priests." And as they went, they were cleansed. One of them, when he saw he was healed, came back, praising God in a loud voice. He threw himself at Jesus' feet and thanked Him—and he was a Samaritan. Jesus asked, "Were not all ten cleansed? Where are the other nine? Has no one returned to give praise to God except this foreigner?" Then He said to him, "Rise and go; your faith has made you well.""

Words Of Encouragement

You have the power to put someone on their feet. You can keep them from falling into depression. You can encourage them to follow their dream. Without your blessing, your encouragement, or your kindness, they won't become what they should have become. Don't miss the opportunity. Take time to be a healer, be a lifter of the people in your life.

"May the Lord now show you kindness and faithfulness, and I too will show you the same favor because you have done this."
(2 Samuel 2:6)

"I thank my God through Jesus Christ for you."
(Romans 1:8)
"I always thank God for you because of his grace given you in Christ Jesus."
(1 Corinthians 1:4)

"I thank God for you—the God I serve with a clear conscience, just as my ancestors did. Night and day I constantly remember you in my prayers." (2 Timothy 1:3)

A Love Letter

Margaret Feinberg stated that when she opened the Bible, she didn't just find instructions for life or a history book, but also discovered a series of love letters. From *Genesis* to *Revelation*, God's love expresses itself in countless ways, stories, and lives. God and His love are manifested in the person of Jesus and demonstrated through His life, death, resurrection, and promise of imminent return.

Why use sixty-six books and thousands of years of history to say three simple words? Because "**I love you**" is not just a piece of information or one-time revelation but an invitation to transformation.

"We give thanks to God always for all of you, constantly mentioning you in our prayers." (1 Thessalonians 1:2)

"The Lord bless you and keep you; The Lord make His face shine upon you, And be gracious to you; The Lord lift up His countenance upon you, And give you peace." (Numbers 6:24-26)

PART 5

SALVATION

CHAPTER 23 - LOST

I PRAY FOR THOSE THAT ARE LOST AND CAN'T FIND THEIR WAY.

Remember *John 3:16* "For God so loved the world that He gave His one and only Son, that whoever believes in Him shall not perish but have eternal life."

And John emphasizes in *verse 18* that "Whoever believes in Him is not condemned, but whoever does not believe stands condemned already because they have not believed in the name of God's one and only Son."

We also see this message in *Romans 8:1* "Therefore, there is now no condemnation for those who are in Christ Jesus," And in *1 John 4:10, 15* "This is love: not that we loved God, but that He loved us and sent His Son as an atoning sacrifice for our sins. If anyone acknowledges that Jesus is the Son of God, God lives in him and he in God."

"For the sake of His great name the Lord will not reject His people, because the Lord was pleased to make you His own. As for me, far be it from me that I should sin against the Lord by failing to pray for you. And I will teach you the way that is good and right."
(1 Samuel 12:22-23)

Shipwrecked

A voyaging ship was wrecked during a storm at sea and only two men were able to swim to a small, desert-like island. The two survivors, not knowing what else to do, agreed that they had no recourse but to pray to God.

However, to find out whose prayer was more powerful, they agreed to divide the territory between them and stay on opposite sides of the island. The first thing they prayed for was food. The next morning, the first man saw a fruit-bearing tree on his side of the land, and he was able to eat its fruit. The other man's parcel of land remained barren.

After a week, the first man was lonely and he decided to pray for a wife. The next day, another ship was wrecked, and the only survivor was a woman who swam to his side of the land. On the other side of the island, there was nothing.

So, on the next day the first man prayed for a house, clothes and more food. The next day, like magic, all of these were given to him. However, the second man still had nothing.

"When I said, "My foot is slipping," Your love, O Lord, supported me. When anxiety was great within me, Your consolation brought joy to my soul." (Psalm 94:18-19)

"Accept one another, then, just as Christ accepted you, in order to bring praise to God." (Romans 15:17)

Finally, the first man prayed for a ship, so that he and his wife could leave the island. In the morning, he found a ship docked at his side of the island. The first man boarded the ship with his wife and decided to leave the second man on the island. He considered the other man unworthy to receive God's blessings, since none of his prayers had been answered.

As the ship was about to leave, the first man heard a voice from Heaven booming, "Why are you leaving your companion on the island?" The first man answered "My blessings are mine alone, since I was the one who prayed for them. His prayers were all unanswered and so he does not deserve anything."

"You are mistaken!" the voice rebuked him. "He had only one prayer, which I answered. If not for that, you would not have received any of my blessings." "Tell me," the first man asked the voice, "What did he pray for that I should owe him anything?" The voice from Heaven stated, "He prayed that all your prayers be answered."

"Take My yoke upon you and learn from Me, for I am gentle and humble in heart, and you will find rest for your souls."
(Matthew 11:29)

"If My people who are called by My name humble themselves, and pray and seek My face, and turn from their wicked ways, then I will hear from heaven, and will forgive their sin and heal their land."
(2 Chronicles 7:14)

CHAPTER 24 - UNDERSTANDING

I PRAY FOR THOSE THAT ARE MISJUDGED AND MISUNDERSTOOD.

Broaden My Mind

As part of our ministerial and theology training years later in the Academy and College, during one quarter we were encouraged to attend a different religious church, temple, mosque or synagogue each Sunday, or Saturday, to thoroughly understand the difference between Lutherans, Catholics, Baptists, Methodists, Jews, Muslims, Buddhists and many others.

As a common theme, each of the religions had their own rituals. But beyond the rituals underlies their belief system.

From what I remember (correct me if I'm wrong), in Judaism, they view salvation as a Judgment Day decision based on their morality and refuse the claim of Christ as the Messiah.

"And He said unto them, Go ye into all the world, and preach the gospel to every creature." *(Mark 16:15)*

"As for me, far be it from me that I should sin against the Lord by failing to pray for you. And I will teach you the way that is good and right." *(1 Samuel 12:23)*

Muslims can only earn their way to Allah by performing the duties of the Five Pillars of Faith. Islam says Jesus was not crucified. Buddhism grades their life according to the Four Noble Truths and the Noble Eightfold Path, looking toward Nirvana, achieved after at least 547 reincarnations. Hindus experience multiple reincarnations in their soul's journey through the cosmos and perceive a plural and impersonal God.

I have often wondered whether it was worth the long-lasting wars, the death of many, and the challenging of religious rituals to attempt the reformation of belief systems around the world. Was the reformation successful or did this effort further divide us?

Protestant Reformation

The Protestant Reformation was the 16th-century religious, political, intellectual and cultural upheaval that splintered Catholic Europe, putting in place the structures and beliefs that define our modern times.

In northern and central Europe, reformers like Martin Luther, John Calvin and Henry VIII challenged papal authority and questioned the Catholic Church's ability to define Christian practice. They argued for a religious and political redistribution of power into the hands of Bible-teaching. The disruption triggered wars, persecutions and the so-called Counter-Reformation of the Catholic Church's response to the Protestants.

Historians usually date the start of the Protestant Reformation to the 1517 publication of Martin Luther's "95 Theses" more than 500 years ago that were posted on the church door in Wittenberg. Its ending can be placed anywhere from the 1555 Peace of Augsburg, which allowed for the coexistence of Catholicism and Lutheranism in Germany, to the 1648 Treaty of Westphalia, which ended the Thirty Years' War. The key ideas of the Reformation were a call to purify the church and a belief that the Bible, not tradition, should be the sole source of spiritual authority.

Martin Luther was an Augustinian monk in Wittenberg when he composed his "95 Theses," which protested the Pope's sale of reprieves from penance, or indulgences. Although he had hoped to spur renewal from within the church, in 1521 he was summoned before the Diet of Worms and excommunicated. Luther translated the Bible into German. He and the other reformers became the first to use the power of the printing press to give their ideas a wide audience. When German peasants revolted in 1524, Luther sided with Germany's princes. By the Reformation's end, Lutheranism had become the state religion throughout much of Germany, Scandinavia and the Baltics.

The Thirty Years' War

Northern Europe's new religious and political freedoms came at a great cost, with decades of rebellions, wars and bloody persecutions. The Thirty Years' War alone cost Germany 40 percent of its population. But the Reformation's positive repercussions can be seen in the intellectual and cultural flourishing it inspired in the strengthened universities of Europe, the Lutheran church music of J.S. Bach, the baroque altarpieces of Pieter Paul Rubens and even the capitalism of Dutch Calvinist merchants.

The Swiss Reformation

The Swiss Reformation began in 1519 with the sermons of Ulrich Zwingli, whose teachings paralleled Luther's. In 1541 John Calvin, a French Protestant who had spent the previous decade in exile writing his "Institutes of the Christian Religion," was invited to settle in Geneva and put his Reformed doctrine, which stressed God's power and humanity's predestined fate, into practice. Calvin's Geneva became a hotbed for Protestant exiles. His doctrines quickly spread to Scotland, France, Transylvania and the Low Countries, where Dutch Calvinism became a religious and economic force for the next 400 years.

English Reformation

In England, the Reformation began with Henry VIII's quest for a male heir. When Pope Clement VII refused to annul Henry's marriage to Catherine of Aragon so he could remarry, the English king declared in 1534 that he alone should be the final authority in matters relating to the English church. Henry dissolved England's monasteries to confiscate their wealth and placed the Bible in the hands of the people. After Henry's death, England tilted toward Calvinist-infused Protestantism during Edward VI's six-year reign and then endured five years of Catholicism under Mary I. In 1559 Elizabeth I took the throne. During her 44-year reign, the Church of England was a "middle way" between Calvinism and Catholicism, with a revised Book of Common Prayer.

Wesleyan Revival

In the 1730s the Evangelical Revival arose in Britain, directed by John Wesley, his brother Charles, and George Whitefield, clergymen in the Church of England.

The Wesleyan phase of the great revival was characterized by three theological landmarks: regeneration by grace through faith; Christian perfection, or sanctification, likewise by grace through faith; and the witness of the Spirit to the assurance of grace. Among John Wesley's distinctive contributions was an emphasis on entire sanctification in this life as God's gracious provision for the Christian.

In October 1895, the Church of the Nazarene was organized as the first denomination that preached entire sanctification received through faith in Christ. They held that Christians sanctified by faith should follow Christ's example and preach the Gospel to the poor. They believed that unnecessary elegance and adornment of houses of worship did not represent the spirit of Christ but the spirit of the world, and that their expenditures of time and money should be given to Christ-like ministries for the salvation of souls and the relief of the needy.

British Methodism

British Methodism's early missionary enterprises began disseminating these theological emphases worldwide. In North America, the Methodist Episcopal Church was organized in 1784.

Its stated purpose was to spread scriptural Holiness over these Lands. In the 19th century a renewed emphasis on Christian holiness began in the Eastern United States and spread throughout the nation.

Presbyterian, Congregational, Baptist

The holiness revival was spread in Presbyterian and Congregationalist circles, as did the holiness movement within the Baptist denomination. The witness to Christian holiness played roles of varying significance in the founding of the Wesleyan Methodist Church (1843), the Free Methodist Church (1860), and, in England, the Salvation Army (1865). In the 1880s new distinctively holiness churches sprang into existence, including the Church of God.

Several older religious traditions were also influenced by the holiness movement, including the Mennonites, Brethren, and Friends that adopted the Wesleyan-holiness view of entire sanctification.

The Catholic Church

The Catholic Church was slow to respond to the theological and publicity innovations of Luther and the other reformers. The Council of Trent defined the Church's answer to the problems that triggered the Reformation. New religious orders, notably the Jesuits, combined spirituality with intellectualism, while mystics such as Teresa of Avila injected new passion into the older orders. Inquisitions, both in Spain and in Rome, were reorganized to fight the threat of Protestant heresy.

Isn't it wonderful that we can all share the same grace of God, the love of Jesus and the renewal of the Holy Spirit?

CHAPTER 25 - INTIMACY

I PRAY FOR THOSE WHO DON'T KNOW YOU INTIMATELY.

Some of us may find that being outdoors with nature or in a church rich in symbols and beauty, is conducive to communing with God. Others have a special place they return to for important times of prayer, a particular chair near the window, or under their favorite tree. They find that doing this helps them center on their relationship with God. It requires self-discipline, adjusted priorities, and relinquishment of old habits to create space for God.

It may be difficult, but it is a great benefit to step off the treadmill of life and attend to things that matter most.

"But thanks be to God, who always leads us in triumphal procession in Christ and through us spreads everywhere the fragrance of the knowledge of Him." (2 Corinthians 2:14)

The Apostles' Creed

The Apostles' Creed, though not written by the apostles, is the oldest creed of the Christian church and is the basis for others that followed. Its most used form is:

> I believe in God the Father Almighty, Maker of heaven and earth, And in Jesus Christ his only Son our Lord, Who was conceived by the Holy Ghost, Born of the Virgin Mary, Suffered under Pontius Pilate, Was crucified, dead, and buried. He descended into hell; The third day He rose again from the dead; He ascended into heaven, And sits on the right hand of God the Father Almighty; From thence he shall come to judge the quick and the dead. I believe in the Holy Ghost; The Holy catholic Church, the Communion of Saints; The Forgiveness of sins; The Resurrection of the body, And the Life everlasting. Amen.

In its oldest form, the Apostles' Creed goes back to at least 140 A.D. Many of the early church leaders summed up their beliefs as they had an opportunity to stand for their faith, for example, *1 Timothy 6:12*. These statements developed into a more standard form to express one's confession of faith at the time of baptism. It is not Scripture, but it is a simple list of the great doctrines of the Christian faith.

"That if you confess with your mouth, "Jesus is Lord," and believe in your heart that God raised Him from the dead, you will be saved. For it is with your heart that you believe and are justified, and it is with your mouth that you confess and are saved." (Romans 10:9-10)

"Fight the good fight of the faith. Take hold of the eternal life to which you were called when you made your good confession in the presence of many witnesses." (1 Timothy 6:12)

The word "catholic" means "relating to the church universal" and was the word used in the original version of the Creed. It does not mean the Roman Catholic Church, but the church, the body of Christ, as a universal fellowship. The phrase, "He descended into hell," was not part of the creed in its earliest form.

Relationships

Relationships are very important. A life without relationships may be a simpler life, but it is also an empty life. The path to the greatest life possible and the greatest joy possible is found in the priority that Jesus taught us to keep at the top of the list. Place the highest value on relationships.

Tom Holladay emphasizes that God created us for relationships. Miss out on relationships, and you're missing the core reason for which God put you on this planet. Jesus knows full well that the wonder and pain of our relationships tempt us to move them down our priority list. "Who needs this?" we say, reducing our lives to simple hobbies, tasks, and entertainments. That's not the answer!

Between You And God

Mother Teresa has been quoted "People are often unreasonable and self-centered. Forgive them anyway. If you are kind, people may accuse you of ulterior motives. Be kind anyway. If you are honest, people may cheat you. Be honest anyway. If you find happiness, people may be jealous. Be happy anyway. The good you do today may be forgotten tomorrow. Do good anyway. Give the world the best you have and it may never be enough. Give your best anyway. For you see, in the end, it is between you and God. It was never between you and them anyway."

CHAPTER 26 - FAITH

I PRAY FOR THOSE THAT DON'T BELIEVE.

Faith - it does not make things easy, it makes them possible. (*Luke 1:37*)

Yes, Virginia

In the 1991 movie "*Yes, Virginia, there is a Santa Claus*" there is one phrase that gets me every time. "How can you believe in something you cannot see?" The response by Virginia is "I believe in God!"

"Yes, Virginia, there is a Santa Claus" is a phrase from an editorial called "Is There a Santa Claus?" that appeared in the September 21, 1897, edition of The New York Sun and has since become part of popular Christmas folklore in the United States. It is the most reprinted newspaper editorial in the English language.

"Whoever believes in Him is not condemned, but whoever does not believe stands condemned already because he has not believed in the name of God's one and only Son."
(John 3:18)

"Whoever believes and is baptized will be saved, but whoever does not believe will be condemned."
(Mark 16:16)

In 1897, Dr. Philip O'Hanlon was asked by his then eight-year-old daughter, Virginia O'Hanlon (1889–1971), whether Santa Claus really existed. O'Hanlon suggested she write to The Sun, assuring her that "If you see it in The Sun, it's so." In so doing, Dr. O'Hanlon had unwittingly given one of the paper's editors, Francis Pharcellus Church, an opportunity to rise above the simple question and address the philosophical issues behind it.

"Whoever acknowledges Me before men, I will also acknowledge him before My Father in heaven. But whoever disowns Me before men, I will disown him before My Father in heaven."
(Matthew 10:32-33)

Church was a war correspondent during the American Civil War, a time that saw great suffering and a corresponding lack of hope and faith in much of society. According to an anecdote on the radio program "The Rest of the Story", Church was a hardened cynic and an atheist who had little patience for superstitious beliefs, did not want to write the editorial, and refused to allow his name to be attached to the piece. More than a century later it is the most reprinted editorial in any newspaper in the English language.

In 1971, after seeing Virginia's obituary in The New York Times, four friends formed a company called Elizabeth Press and published a children's book titled "Yes, Virginia". Its creators took it to Warner Brothers, who eventually made an Emmy award-winning television show based on the editorial.

The History Channel, in a special that aired on February 21, 2001, noted that Virginia gave the original letter to a granddaughter, who pasted it in a scrapbook. It was feared that the letter was destroyed in a house fire but, 30 years later, it was discovered intact.

Every year, Virginia's letter and Church's response are read at the Yule Log ceremony at Church's alma mater, Columbia College of Columbia University.

Innocence

The story's ability to enchant readers has to do with the attraction we have for childhood innocence. More than being a tactful reply to a delicate question, Mr. Church was somehow able to explain the fundamental nature of innocence and how it helps the person see a higher reality.

This was the opinion of a Catholic thinker Prof. Plinio Correa de Oliveira. He defined innocence as "the desire… to know God from the reflection in His creatures." This is the essence of Mr. Church's reply to Virginia.

"The most real things in the world", Mr. Church says, "are those that neither children nor men can see." Santa might not exist, he explained, but the "love, generosity and devotion" he represents certainly does.

"It is impossible for those who have once been enlightened, who have tasted the heavenly gift, who have shared in the Holy Spirit, who have tasted the goodness of the Word of God and the powers of the coming age, if they fall away, to be brought back to repentance, because to their loss they are crucifying the Son of God all over again and subjecting him to public disgrace."
(Hebrews 6:4-6)

More than Santa, Church assures the reader that love, good, and all manner of unseen wonders, including God, exist and will continue to exist.

Children therefore are able to see God when He is aptly symbolized in things that surround them, even Santa Claus.

At the same time, every Christmas we read a similar story from the Bible "Yes, Virginia, there is a God. He came to earth as a humble baby named Jesus to save us from our sins."

More than wanting to know if there is a Santa, Virginia wanted to know if there is a God. With this in mind we can categorically affirm, as we commemorate His birth, "Yes, Virginia there is a God." The universe literally screams of His existence but only for those who have eyes to see. Paraphrasing Mr. Church we can more accurately say about God, "He lives and lives forever. A thousand years from now, Virginia, nay 10 times 10,000 years from now, He will continue to make glad the heart of childhood."

"The faithless will be fully repaid for their ways, and the good man rewarded for his."
(Proverbs 14:14)

"For the grace of God has appeared that offers salvation to all people. It teaches us to say "No" to ungodliness and worldly passions, and to live self-controlled, upright and godly lives in this present age,"
(Titus 2:11-12)

The Fiery Furnace

When my children were very young, I had the honor of putting them to bed on occasion. This is no easy task for any parent – with "I'm thirsty", "I'm not tired" and any number of excuses. We tried bribery, threats and even games. For one of these games, I would hug them and throw them (gracefully) into bed as I said "Shadrach, Meshach and To Bed We Go".

In the book of Daniel we read the story of three men in a fiery furnace. King Nebuchadnezzar had made an image of gold and required everyone to fall down and worship the image when they heard musical instruments play. Shadrach, Meshach and Abednego paid no attention to serving the King's gods nor did they worship the image of gold.

"But the day of the Lord will come like a thief. The heavens will disappear with a roar; the elements will be destroyed by fire, and the earth and everything done in it will be laid bare. Since everything will be destroyed in this way, what kind of people ought you to be?"
(2 Peter 3:10-11)

The King proclaimed that if they did not worship the image, they would be thrown immediately into a blazing furnace. These three men responded that, if they were thrown into the blazing furnace, the God they served is able to deliver them from the burning furnace, but even if He did not, they would not serve the King's gods or worship the image of gold. The King was furious.

So these three men, wearing their robes, trousers, turbans and other clothes, were bound and thrown into the blazing furnace. The King was amazed and said "I see four men walking around in the fire, unbound and unharmed, and the fourth looks like a son of the gods." Then Nebuchadnezzar said, "Praise be to the God of Shadrach, Meshach and Abednego, who has sent His angel and rescued His servants! They trusted in Him and defied the king's command and were willing to give up their lives rather than serve or worship any god except their own God." (*Daniel 3:28*) What a demonstration of faith!

Paganism

In the Old Testament, the Babylonians worshiped Marduk. They also worshiped Molech, Ashtoreth and many others. For many centuries before Israel entered the land of Palestine, ancient Canaanite fertility cults used child sacrifices and same-sex rituals to worship their false gods. God prohibited Israel from adopting the cultic, sexual, fertility goddess worship of Egypt and Canaan in *Leviticus 18:3* and in chapter *20: 22-23*.

Organized paganism can be seen throughout all biblical times. King Xerxes worshiped Ahura-Mazda referenced in the book of *Esther* (a deity from Middle-Eastern mythology, a bright and beautiful Zoroastrian Supreme god that is still worshiped today as the creator of the universe and source of all good things). He is so bright that a certain brand of electric light bulb is named in his honor.

Molech was the national deity of the Ammonites, a fire god. Children were sacrificed to it. Ashtoreth was the fertility and war goddess consort of Molech. The religious Canaanites of Palestine worshiped this fertility goddess also. Many temples were built to ancient gods. Take a look at the Golden Calf in *Exodus 32*. Or how about ancient gods like the goat-demons and desert satyrs found in *Leviticus 17*.

We see that civil and moral laws were introduced in Moses time. Clean and unclean food (*Leviticus 11:1-42*), child sacrifices (*Leviticus 18:21*), unlawful sexual relations such as homosexuality (*Leviticus 18:22*) and the Ten Commandments (*Exodus 20:2-17, Leviticus 19:1-37* and *Deuteronomy 5:6-21*).

Some 1450 years later we find Rome as the sewer of humanity. The ancient custom of shrine prostitution, prevalent in first century Rome, forms the historical motif of *Romans 1*. Ancient shrine prostitution is the most historically accurate explanation of Paul's words in the first chapter of *Romans*. So, during the life of Jesus, we find many false gods and paganism. The current day Spanish fountain in Rome honors Cybele, an ancient fertility goddess and protector of Rome, whose pagan temple loomed over first century Rome from atop the Palatine Hill.

Unbelievers

Many Biblical references can be made about unbelievers. Apostle Paul writes about idols and images in *Romans 1:22-23*, men and homosexuality in *Romans 1:24-27*, the law giving sin its power over us and legalism being the arch enemy of holiness (*1 Corinthians 15:56*). The high regard for the Torah in Judaism made it difficult to grasp Paul's "law-free" gospel (*Acts 14-15*). "Therefore, there is now no condemnation for those who are in Christ Jesus, because through Christ Jesus the law of the Spirit of Life set me free from the law of sin and death" (*Romans 8:1*). All of salvation – justification, reconciliation, sanctification and eternal life – flow from God's grace, His unmerited favor.

Almost 2000 years later (current day), we find spiritual challenges in our schools, public offices, monetary system "In God We Trust", abortion issues and Proposition 102 dealing with marriage as a union between one man and one women.

"If my people, who are called by My Name, will humble themselves and pray and seek My face and turn from their wicked ways, then I will hear from heaven, and I will forgive their sin and heal their land." (*2 Chronicles 7:14*) Scary world we live in now but we must not give in to "fear", that is what the evil doers want. We must turn back to God! We need Him to heal our land for the future generations.

Prepare

"No eye has seen, no ear has heard, no mind has conceived what God has prepared for those who love Him, but God has revealed it to us by his Spirit." – (*1 Corinthians 2:9*). Paul tells us that the Spirit of God searches all things, even the deep things of God.

Wisdom is given through the Spirit. "The man without the Spirit does not accept the things that come from the Spirit of God, for they are foolishness to him, and he cannot understand them, because they are spiritually discerned." (*1 Corinthians 2:14*) We must mature in God's wisdom that He has destined for our glory.

Only the blood of Jesus Christ, shed on the cross two thousand years ago, protects us from the judgment of God for sin. We are not justified because of our good deeds. We are not protected because of our appeals. We can do nothing to merit God's favor. Only the blood puts us in right standing with Him. In the words of the Andraé Crouch song often sung in church, the blood of Jesus "reaches to the highest mountain" and "flows to the lowest valley." That is why "it will never lose its power."

Mustard Seed

The Parable of the Mustard Seed is one of the shorter parables of Jesus. It appears in *Matthew 13:31–32, Mark 4:30–32,* and *Luke 13:18–19.* In the Gospels of *Matthew* and *Luke,* it is followed by the Parable of the Leaven, which shares this parable's theme of the Kingdom of Heaven growing from small beginnings. This parable also suggests the growth of the kingdom of God from tiny beginnings. It also appears in the non-canonical Gospel of Thomas verse 20.

The mustard plant referred to is considered to be black mustard, a large annual plant up to 9 feet tall, growing from a small seed in fields and seldom in gardens due to its size. This small mustard seed is also used to refer to faith in *Matthew 17:20* and *Luke 17:6.*

Faith is vital to the Christian life. Scripture tells us that, without it, it is impossible to please God (*Hebrews 11:6*). Yet faith is such a powerful gift from God (*Ephesians 2:8–9*) Christ told His disciples that with just a tiny measure of faith, the size of a mustard seed, they could move mountains. So, what does it mean to have "mustard seed faith"?

The reference to "mustard seed faith" is seen twice in Scripture. First, in *Matthew 17:14–20,* Christ's disciples are unable to exorcise a demon from a young boy, even though Jesus had given them authority to do this. (*Matthew 10:1*) When they asked Jesus why they were not able to drive out the demon, Jesus replied, "Because you have so little faith. I tell you the truth, if you have faith as small as a mustard seed, you can say to this mountain, 'move from here to there' and it will move; nothing will be impossible for you." (*Matthew 17:14–20*)

Next, in *Luke 17:6*, Jesus tells His disciples, "If you have faith as small as a mustard seed, you can say to this mulberry tree, 'Be uprooted and planted in the sea,' and it will obey you." By using the mustard seed example, Jesus is speaking about the incalculable power of God when unleashed in the lives of those with true faith.

The power of faith reflects the omnipotent nature of the God who bestows faith on His own. The mustard seed is one of the tiniest seeds found in the Middle East, so the conclusion is that the amount of faith needed to do great things is very small indeed.

Jesus uses the mustard seed reference to make the point that little is much when it comes from God. The mustard seed in the parable grows to be a huge tree, representing the tiny beginnings of Christianity when just a few disciples began to preach and teach the gospel. Eventually, the kingdom grew to huge proportions, encompassing the entire world and spreading over centuries.

So, too, does the tiniest bit of faith, when it is true faith from God, grow to immense proportions in the lives of believers and spreading out to influence all those that they come into contact with. One has only to read histories of the great men of the faith to know that superhuman feats were performed by those whose faith was, at one time, only the size of a mustard seed.

PART 6

FAMILY VALUES

CHAPTER 27 - CHANGE

I BELIEVE THAT GOD CHANGES PEOPLE AND GOD CHANGES THINGS.

Apostle Paul writes "And we know that in all things God works for the good of those who love Him, who have been called according to His purpose." (*Romans 8:28*)

Purpose

After 37 years of working for the same employer, the company underwent downsizing. I was one of the casualties. During this same period, my wife was diagnosed as chronic depressive after her hysterectomy, my father-in-law became very ill and had multiple leg amputations caused by diabetes, my middle son had gone off to fight the Desert Storm war in the Navy and my oldest son was diagnosed as a manic-depressive with multiple suicidal attempts. Needless to say, there was stress in our lives – but God watched over us and gave us strength as He promised in *Matthew 6:34* – "Therefore do not worry about tomorrow, for tomorrow will worry about itself. Each day has enough trouble of its own."

"But we ought always to thank God for you, brothers loved by the Lord, because from the beginning God chose you to be saved through the sanctifying work of the Spirit and through belief in the truth." (2 Thessalonians 2:13)

"But show me unfailing kindness like that of the Lord as long as I live." (1 Samuel 20:14)

Although my employment had been terminated, I felt that this was actually a blessing because I had always wanted to start my own consulting business. An additional opportunity presented itself to start a second business at the same time. I partnered with what I thought to be Christians. Capital was raised, employees hired and a software product was being developed by a programmer from India, and another from Pakistan. Marketing and sales initiatives had begun. My daughter became one of our employees.

I was making several business trips trying to sell our software product. On one business trip I flew from Minnesota to Michigan. I had an appointment to make a large sale to a major airport and to the city government. That happened to be the morning of September 11, 2001. Guess what! Not only were the appointments canceled, but the airport was shut down and no rental vehicles could be found because they were all being reserved for the Red Cross during this 9/11 disaster. That terrorist incident left me stranded for a couple of days. My daughter-in-law was able to get me a train ticket for the following day, just so I could get home.

"Do not say, "Why were the old days better than these?" For it is not wise to ask such questions. When times are good, be happy; but when times are bad, consider: God has made the one as well as the other. Therefore, a man cannot discover anything about his future." (Ecclesiastes 7:10, 14)

Driving home from another business trip in Michigan, I started to have some severe pains in my lower back. It was a long drive home, so I stopped at a McDonalds at about 10 p.m. to rest. I tried to get out of the car to walk around a bit, but the pain was so severe by this time that I could not move.

I could see an employee inside cleaning up and motioned several times for her to come to my aid. Hesitantly, she came out and I asked her to call for medical assistance.

It took four paramedics to get me out of the car. They transported me to a hospital. I called my wife, who in turn, called my son, to come and get me. Morphine wasn't cutting the pain. When we arrived home, both of my sons had to carry me into the house. What I found out was that I had a ruptured disk in my lower back. After surgery the doctor told me that the disk had shattered, with fragments floating in the spinal fluid. God surely blessed me with His healing. A few days in the hospital and I walked out on my own accord.

Shortly after that, however, the software business was starting to take a turn for the worst. Motivation of some owners had changed from passion to that of greed. We were not raising more capital, we were not selling more software, our funds were depleted, and I had no more income.

We soon had to sell our house before we lost it. In addition, I was begging and borrowing in order to pay medical insurance premiums. My wife was a diabetic, was still in depression and going blind. She had a couple of eye surgeries without success. The doctor refused to perform any more surgeries. My oldest son gratefully purchased our home (with his wife and three children) and we moved to a rental townhouse from the proceeds of the sale.

Praying For Change

During the first part of that year I received unemployment benefits from the state while I searched for any income opportunity.

While waiting for any opportunity, I had set up the garage as my woodworking shop and began making various items like the bathroom vanity for my sons' house; the custom mission-style stair railing and the 6-drawer bed frame for my daughter.

After one year I was still not employed and our funds had totally run out. Our middle son offered to take us in. (He had four boys of his own.) It took another 9 months before I received a phone call for a temporary 6 week consulting contract assignment. Of course I accepted. After the six weeks, they renewed the contract for another 6 months. They finally offered me a full time position under one condition. I had to relocate – either to Ft. Lauderdale, Florida or Phoenix, Arizona.

After living in Minnesota my whole life, I didn't like the humidity, mosquitoes, tornadoes, snow, ice and 20 below zero. I had been to Florida on business trips multiple times and didn't like the humidity, nor the thoughts of hurricanes. I had driven through Phoenix once, when our middle son was on his way to Japan from San Diego in the Navy. All I remember was that it was hot (120 degrees that day) and the car air conditioner wasn't working. To make this decision, we prayed for God's direction in our lives.

Old Weathered Barn

I once heard the story of an old weathered barn. "A stranger came by the other day with an offer that set me to thinking. He wanted to buy the old barn that sits out by the highway. I told him right off he was crazy. He was a city type. You could tell by his clothes, his car, his hands, and the way he talked.

He said he was driving by and saw that beautiful old barn sitting out in the tall grass and wanted to know if it was for sale. I told him he had a funny idea of beauty. Sure, it was a handsome building in its day. But then, there's been a lot of winters pass with their snow and ice and howling wind. The summer sun's beat down on that ole' barn till all the paint's gone, and the wood has turned silver gray.

Now the old building leans a good deal, looking kind of tired. Yet, that fellow called it beautiful.

That set me to thinking. I walked out to the field and just stood there, gazing at the old barn. The fellow said he planned to use the lumber to line the walls of his den in a new country home he's building down the road. He said you couldn't get paint that beautiful. Only years of standing in the weather, bearing the storms and scorching sun...only that can produce beautiful barn wood.

It came to me then. We are a lot like that, you and I. Only it's on the inside the beauty grows with us. Sure, we turn silver gray too...and lean a bit more than we did when we were young and full of sap. But the Good Lord knows what He is doing. And as the years pass He's busy using the hard wealth of our lives, the dry spells, and the stormy seasons, to do a job of beautifying our souls that nothing else can produce. And to think how often folks holler because they want life easy!

They took the old barn down today and hauled it away to beautify a rich man's house. And I reckon that you and I'll be hauled off to Heaven to take on whatever chores the Good Lord has for us in the Great Sky Ranch. And I suspect we'll be more beautiful then for the seasons we've been through here...and just maybe add a bit of beauty to our Father's house."

Fanny Crosby

An excerpt from the *New Women's Devotional Bible* tells the story of Fanny Crosby. "She was not content to be a victim. She voraciously memorized five books of the Old Testament and most of the New Testament by the time she was ten years old. She attended the New York Institute for the Blind, where she became a teacher and gifted poet. After surviving the cholera epidemic in 1849, Fanny realized something was missing in her life and turned to Christ at the age of 30. God had been silently working in her heart.

The poetry that formerly flowed from her heart turned into hymns of praise, many of which we still sing today.

In *Genesis 41* we see God silently working in Joseph's life. Joseph could have grown bitter and inflamed by the dreadful circumstances of his life. But amazingly, Joseph experienced God's silent work as much in slavery and in prison as he did when he rose to prominence.

Whatever your circumstances, you can trust that God is working behind the scenes. When you experience trouble—and you will—God can make you fruitful and full of praise, just as he did with Joseph and with Fanny Crosby."

May there be peace within you today. May you trust God that you are exactly where you are meant to be.

CHAPTER 28 –
SISTERS AND
BROTHERS

I PRAY FOR ALL MY SISTERS AND BROTHERS.

There is nothing more important than family. It means that you belong. A family can be blood-relatives, adopted or foster children needing a home, a family of fellow workers, or even a family of believers. They are all brothers and sisters in Christ. They are what bring warmth to your heart.

"Dear friend, I pray that you may enjoy good health and that all may go well with you, even as your soul is getting along well."
(3 John 1:2)

My Sisters

I can remember playing with my sisters in blanket forts using chairs and a card table covered with blankets. I remember steaming under a blanket when we were sick, and the time we decided to run away from home. My sisters and I would spend hours collecting acorns in brown paper bags from the three big Oak trees in our front yard on Colfax.

In the 4th grade we moved into a new house. My sisters and I attended a public school at the top of a hill in our neighborhood. (I found out later in life that my daughter's mother-in-law taught at that school.)We would walk up the hill to our school, but when it rained, the wet mud-clay soil was too much for us. We would constantly loose our boots. I can remember a student in my class, David C., who pulled a knife on our teacher.

"And whatever you ask in prayer, you will receive, if you have faith." (Matthew 21:22)

One day when it was raining, we looked out of our living room window and saw a large earthmover sink in front of our eyes. It was never removed. Another day we saw our neighbor's cesspool disappear in their front yard.

My sisters and I would sell lemonade to the construction workers in the summer, play with salamanders in the back yard and make mud pies. There was a park at the bottom of the hill where we would play on the slide, swings and a crazy spinning thing.

We would practice our tennis swings by hitting the tennis balls against the back of the house. Dad would get a little upset because we were cracking the siding. We also enjoyed jumping over the small evergreen next to the garage and rolling down the hills on both sides of our house.

We even practiced our juggling skills in the basement. Mom and dad had given us a plastic bowling set as an Easter gift. And of course, as kids, we soon became bored with bowling.

However, the pins were just the right size for juggling. It didn't take long to discover that the basement ceiling was very low and that the plastic bowling pins could actually crack the glass in the recessed lighting fixture. (Years later I had an opportunity to revisit that house. The crack was still in the ceiling fixture.)

I was just learning how to play the guitar at that time. When my sisters were doing the supper dishes, I would sit at the kitchen table and play various songs, and they would sing some beautiful harmony. They both had great voices.

Church Worship

I had a passion for Sunday school, Church and Bible stories so much that, when I was 10 years old, my sisters and I would set up small chairs in our living room. The chairs were perfectly lined up in two rows. They would place their dolls and teddy bears on those chairs, we would sing hymns and I would stand facing the chairs and practice the Sunday Liturgy from the front of our Lutheran Hymnal. These included many Gregorian chants as well as the Lord's Prayer and Apostle's Creed. My parents and grandmother thought it was cute.

The Lutheran Hymnal (TLH) is one of the official hymnals of the Lutheran Church–Missouri Synod (LCMS). Published by Concordia Publishing House in St. Louis, Missouri, it became the common hymnal for both the LCMS and the Wisconsin Evangelical Lutheran Synod (WELS).It contained 668 chorales, hymns, carols, and chants, plus the liturgy for the Common Service, Matins, Vespers, the Proper's, Collects and Prayers, the Suffrages, Canticles and Psalms. TLH became an extremely popular and beloved worship resource in the Lutheran church in North America, and attempts to succeed it in more recent years have often met with strong resistance.

Reverend Billy Graham once wrote a response to a question regarding the introduction of new songs into the church service. To paraphrase, he said that "... we have a singing faith, and God has given us the gift of music to praise Him. The Psalmist declared, 'With singing lips my mouth will praise you' (*Psalm 63.5*)."

"I urge you to ask God to help you be grateful for all music that points us to God, new or old. You may not like some of it, but others do, and God can use it in their lives to encourage them and bring them closer to Christ. Remember: The old hymns you like were once new, and someone probably didn't like them either.

A hymn can become so familiar to us that we sing it without even thinking about the words, which can make our singing empty and meaningless. Meditate on the words of the songs you sing, and even turn them into a prayer."

"Praise Him with the sounding of the trumpet,   praise Him with the harp and lyre, praise Him with timbrel and dancing, praise Him with the strings and pipe, praise Him with the clash of cymbals, praise Him with resounding cymbals." (*Psalm 150:3-5*)

Family

Until I was three years old, our family lived in a military prefabricated metal 2 bedroom Quonset house duplex in North Minneapolis, Minnesota where my younger twin sisters and I were born shortly after World War II. Then our family moved in with our grandparents' into a white two-story house on Fremont Avenue. These were my mom's parents. The second-floor bathroom had those small octagon-shaped white porcelain tiles on the walls and floor. It had a coal-burning furnace. My grandparents would let me watch as the coal truck opened the chute to the basement and the black dust would billow into the air as the coal bin was filled. During the evening, we would sit in the living room to listen to their favorite radio show – "Fibber McGee and Molly".

By the time I started kindergarten, we had moved to a new house on Perry Avenue. Both Grandma and Grandpa moved with us to this house. I can remember walking to school with my lunch box and nap mat. My dad got a new job with Schweigert's Meat Company delivering wholesale meats to hospitals, schools and restaurants around the Twin Cities. He worked 10 hour days, 6 days a week. Because of this, it was in this house that we could afford our first black and white Zenith television. We were allowed to watch "Lawrence Welk", "Mitch Miller", "You Asked for It", "Sea Hunt" and "Lassie" when the doors of the TV cabinet were opened.

My mother became a real estate agent when we lived in this house. (She never sold a house, but each house she listed, she bought.) We then moved three blocks north and one block west to a stucco house on Orchard Avenue with a cyclone fence and weeping willows in the back yard (staying there for only one month because of the ants) and finally moving to another house on Knox Avenue with the red brick exterior and pillars guarding the porch. My grandparents moved with us each time.

During the winter of February 1st, 1953, while in first grade, an uninsured drivers' car hit me as I crossed the street while walking home from parochial school. I can still remember the Police Officer bringing me home to our house. I remember my Grandmother tending to the blood on my face while my mother called the ambulance. I was in the hospital for an entire week. The doctors determined that I had a hairline fracture on the back of my skull.

I was enrolled at Earl Brown public school in the 2nd grade after we moved to a new house on Colfax Avenue. We had a phone installed – complete with a party line and I remember when doctors and TV repair men would make house calls. This house was on a corner lot with three big oak trees in the front yard. That's where I learned to ride a bike, started Cub Scouts, made my first pinewood derby car, and learned how to grow gladiolas in the garden and basic woodworking skills taught by my grandfather.

This is also where I had my first girlfriend – Susanne B. It was in this house where my grandmother taught me to darn my own socks. On Saturdays we were allowed to watch television – "Howdy Dowdy", "Rin Tin Tin", "Sky King", "Roy Rogers", the "Lone Ranger" and "Superman". The TV repairman would even come to the house to replace vacuum tubes when necessary.

Almost every year our family would drive to northern Minnesota to see my mom's sister and our cousins. I remember driving the tractor, bailing alfalfa and feeding the beef cattle. We would visit with our cousins and put on a play for our parents by standing on the stairway leading to the upstairs bedrooms. I remember singing "The milk in the pail goes ping, ping, ping …"We would spend time at Sawyers Resort where my folks would rent a log cabin, sometimes with our Aunt and Uncle and our cousins, and visit the Mississippi River headwaters and Itasca State Park.

As a special treat after church services, our family would go to a Chinese-American restaurant on Broadway to have Midwestern-style chow mein made with celery covering crispy noodles and a side of white rice and, of course, the fortune cookie. With the seven of us (mom, dad, grandparents and 3 kids) we had to sit at the only large table right by the basement staircase. I usually ended up sitting next to that door, thinking that some magical creature might appear at any moment.

Fellow Workers
The moving company delivered our furniture and belongings five days after we moved to Arizona. Since we were new to the area, we had not yet met anyone. I had already started my new job, and we had been sleeping on an air mattress lying on the floor that was only partially inflated.

We had purchased this brand new air mattress in a box that claimed to have a self-contained battery-operated motor that would inflate the mattress in five minutes. After installing the batteries, and with anxious anticipation, the mattress started to inflate. Then, without hesitation, we could hear a rattling sound within the motor. The plastic fan blades began to split and break apart. There was nothing we could do. The motor could run all day long, but without fan blades the mattress would never fully inflate. Since the motor was self-contained, it could not even be bypassed to manually inflate the mattress. Have you ever tried to sleep on a partially filled air mattress with two people?

The day the truck arrived was the same day that I was determined to at least get our queen-sized mattress off of the truck. Now, at that time, I was still a rather sickly individual, only 123 pounds and suffering from C.O.P.D. I crawled into the truck and tugged at the mattress. After many attempts, I was finally able to get it off the truck and onto the blacktop road. (By the way, this was about 4:00 pm in Phoenix the first week of July. The temperature was only 112 degrees that day.) I could not move the mattress any further. A neighbor was watching from across the street. She and her daughter came over and asked if I could use some help. I gladly accepted. (I found out later that this neighbor lady was 82 years old at that time.)

The next day I asked my boss if he knew of anyone that unloaded furniture. He immediately sent an email and, within minutes, stated that there would be helpers available on Saturday morning. To our surprise, all the employees in my department showed up and unloaded the truck in less than three hours. What a blessing to have brothers and sisters that you didn't even know existed.

Jesus Family
Mark 3:35 tells us that "Whoever does God's will is my brother and sister and mother."

I am intrigued with researching my family tree. So far I have identified over 4,000 individuals. Most of these families originally came from Germany.

So, did Jesus have brothers and sisters? For centuries theologians have debated whether or not Jesus had any siblings. But what does scripture say about this complicated family tree?

Four men - James (the Just), Joseph (Joses), Judas (Jude, Judah), Simon (Simeon) and two women are referenced in the Bible as Jesus siblings, both brothers and sisters.

The four men—James, Joses, Simon, and Judas—are mentioned as the brothers or siblings of Jesus in *Matthew 13:55* and *Mark 6:3*. There has been much discussion through the centuries as to the exact relationship of these men to Jesus. So the question remains, did Jesus have siblings? Three principal views have been offered:

1. That they were Jesus' actual siblings/brothers, that is, half-brothers, sons of Joseph and Mary (and therefore younger than Jesus);

2. That they were His stepbrothers, that is, children of Joseph by a previous marriage (and thus all older than He and not His blood relatives at all);

3. That they were the cousins of Jesus on the mother's side, according to some, or on Joseph's side, according to others.

Those who hold the first view argue that this is the most natural way to understand the various references to these brothers; also that this is the most obvious intent of *Matthew 1:25* and *Luke 2:7*.

Those who hold the second view argue that family ethics would not permit younger siblings to taunt or otherwise meddle with an older brother as Jesus' brothers taunted Him (see *Mark 3:31* and *John 7:3-4*). They point out further that the fact that Jesus left His mother in the care of the apostle John (*John 19:26-27*) rather than with one of His brothers strongly implies that Mary had no other children.

The view that these brothers were the cousins of Jesus on Joseph's side is based on pure conjecture. That they were cousins on Mary's side is based on the unproved identity of "Mary, the wife of Cleophus" with the sister of Mary (*John 19:25* and *Mark 15:40*), and on the unproved identity of "Clopas" with Alphaeus (*Mark 3:18*).

Jesus' siblings are mentioned as accompanying Jesus and his mother to Capernaum after the marriage at Cana (*John 2:12*). Later Mary and these brothers are recorded as seeking an audience with Jesus (*Matthew 12:46-50, Mark 3:31-35* and *Luke 8:19-21*). Toward the end of Jesus' ministry, His brethren are mentioned as urging Jesus to prove His Messiahship, which they themselves doubted (*John 7:3-5*). That they were later converted is clear, for they are described in Acts as uniting with the disciples and others in "prayer and supplication" prior to Pentecost (*Acts 1:13-14*). Paul implies that they were all married (*1 Corinthians 9:5*).

Many commentators hold that the author of the epistle of Jude, who identifies himself as the "brother of James," was one of these brothers (*Jude 1*). It is also generally believed that the leader of the church at Jerusalem was James the brother of Jesus, (see *Acts 12:17* and *15:13*). This seems to be confirmed by Paul's reference to his visit to Jerusalem, in which he states that he saw only Peter, and "James, the Lord's brother" (*Galatians 1:18-19*).

So, let's look at the family tree of Jesus having at least six siblings. These included his brothers James, Joseph, Simon, and Judas as well as at least two sisters. (*Matthew 13:54-56* and *Mark 6:3*) Those siblings may have been natural children of Jesus' mother, Mary, and her husband, Joseph. (*Matthew 1:25*) The New Testament names James the Just, Joses, Simon, and Jude as the brothers (Greek *adelphoi*) of Jesus (*Mark 6:3, Matthew 13:55, John 7:3, Acts 1:14,* and *1 Corinthians 9:5*) Another verse in the Epistle to the *Galatians 1:19* mentions seeing James, "the Lord's brother", The Bible calls Jesus "the firstborn" of Mary, which implies that she had other children.—*Luke 2:7*.

Many believe that the Greek word (Greek 'ἀδελφοί', Roman. 'adelphoi', literal. 'brothers') makes reference to these brothers and sisters as a special designation because of their close association with the nuclear family of Jesus, and are actually either his cousins or children of Joseph from a previous marriage.

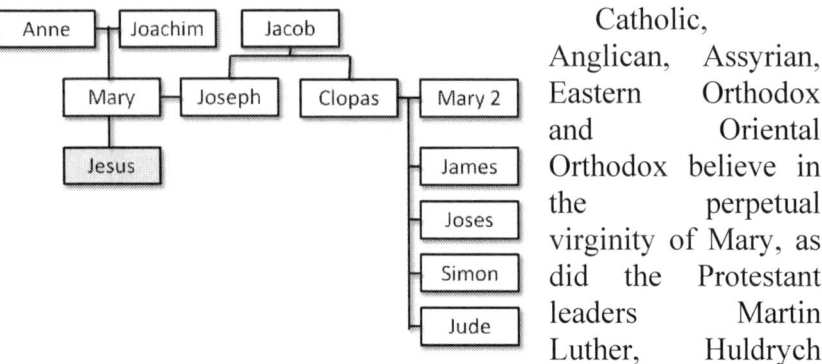

Catholic, Anglican, Assyrian, Eastern Orthodox and Oriental Orthodox believe in the perpetual virginity of Mary, as did the Protestant leaders Martin Luther, Huldrych Zwingli, John Wesley and their respective movements; John Calvin believed that it was possible that Mary remained a virgin but believed the scriptural evidence was inconclusive. Those who hold this belief reject the claim that Jesus had biological siblings and maintain that these brothers and sisters received this designation because of their close association with the nuclear family of Jesus, and are actually either his cousins or children of Joseph from a previous marriage.

The apocryphal 'History of Joseph the Carpenter', written in the 5th century and framed as a biography of Joseph dictated by Jesus, describes how Joseph had with his first wife four sons and two daughters. His sons' names were Judas, Justus, James, and Simon and the names of the two daughters were Assia and Lydia. Years after his first wife died he took Mary. Therefore, the brothers of Jesus would be the children of Joseph by his first wife.

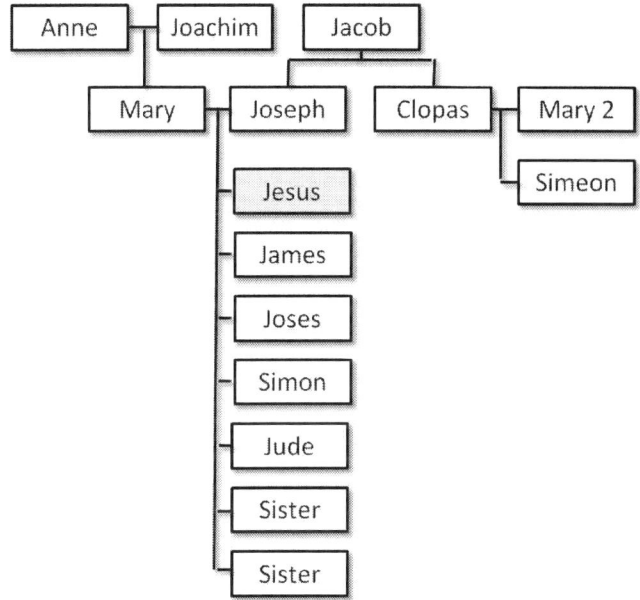

Jesus may have acted like an only child at times in the gospels, but all of the four evangelists make some mention of his brothers and sisters. In Mark, a crowd asks of Jesus, "Is not this the carpenter, the son of Mary and brother of James and Joses and Judas and Simon, and are his sisters here with us?" (*Mark 6:3*).

A similar reference occurs earlier in *Mark 3:31*—"His mother and brothers arrived...." In Luke, when Jesus is told by a crowd gathered to hear him speak, "Your mother and your brothers are standing outside, wanting to see you," Jesus famously rejects them: "My mother and my brothers are those who hear the word of God and do it" (*Luke 8:19-21*). And John writes that after Jesus performed his first miracles in Cana, "he went down to Capernaum with his mother, his brothers, and his disciples; and they remained there a few days" (*Luke 2:12*). *Matthew 1:18 and 25* are very clear about their relationship after Jesus birth. *Matthew. 12: 46-50, Matthew. 13:53-57* and *John. 2:11-12* also speak of his brothers and sisters. Even *Jude 1:*1 claims that he is the brother of James.

John 19:26-27 When Jesus saw his mother standing there beside the disciple He loved, He said to her, "Dear woman, here is your son." And he said to this disciple, "Here is your mother." And from then on this disciple took her into his home. James and Joseph (called Jesus' "brothers" in *Mark 6:3*) are indeed children of Mary.

It does get a little confusing when you look further into Scripture.

Those who were called the brothers and sisters of Jesus may actually have been children of Mary's sister, another Mary, whom he considered the wife of Clopas. James and Joses were the sons of Mary of Clophas (*Mark 15:40*). Judas was the son of James (not either of the Apostles) (*Luke 6:16*). James the Lesser was the son of Alphaeus (*Luke 6:15*). James the Greater and John were the sons of Zebedee with a mother other than Jesus' mother Mary (*Matthew 20:20*).

The Catholic Encyclopedia cites texts contained in the apocryphal writings that:

When forty years of age, Joseph married a woman called Melcha or Escha by some, Salome by others; they lived forty-nine years together and had six children, two daughters and four sons, the youngest of whom was James (the Less, "the Lord's brother"). A year after his wife's death, as the priests announced through Judea that they wished to find in the tribe of Juda a respectable man to espouse Mary, then twelve to fourteen years of age. Joseph, who was at the time ninety years old, went up to Jerusalem among the candidates; a miracle manifested the choice God had made of Joseph, and two years later the Annunciation took place.

So, Jesus had four brothers and at least two sisters. They could either be Jesus' younger brothers and sisters, older half-brothers and half-sisters who were children of Joseph from an earlier marriage, or his cousins. Although we cannot be absolutely certain, the natural sense in which to take the references is they were his actual younger brothers and sisters.

John tells us that during the ministry of Jesus "even His brothers did not believe in Him" (*John 7:5*). Later, however, they became active leaders in the church with two of them (James and Jude) writing letters that became part of the New Testament.

This would seem to indicate actual brothers, other children of Joseph and Mary, rather than stepbrothers. But one cannot be absolutely certain. What is certain, however, is that the Scripture does not rule out the possibility of Jesus having brothers and sisters born to Joseph and Mary.

This issue will continue to be discussed until the end of time. But, does it really matter? We are all brothers and sisters in God's sight.

Friendship

You meet many people along the pathway of your life journey. Some are from your childhood, your school, others from work, and many through Christian fellowship. I believe that friends are quiet angels who lift us to our feet when our wings have trouble remembering how to fly.

I remember being adventurous with a couple of neighborhood friends around the age of eight. During winter break, we walked down to a swamp area to explore. The water had well frozen over - we thought. Well, a couple steps across the swamp and I broke through the ice. After my friends pulled me out, I was very cold and still had to walk home with frozen pants.

Since I lived in a campus dormitory during high school - Luther Hall at Concordia Academy, it was easy to start your own band. You could always hear guitars playing folk songs from "Peter, Paul and Mary" or "Herman's Hermits" – even mine. Many of the students came from other states. I was kind of lucky, because my home was only about 30 miles away. Grandma always had a 'care package' for me, loaded with chocolate chip cookies and brownies, to take back to the dorm every Sunday night.

It didn't take too long for the guys to start coming home with me on weekends. They would enjoy all the baked goods that Grandma would make. Of course they would bring their dirty laundry with them, since my mom and Grandma 'volunteered' to do it for them.

Reflecting back through the years, I have always been an introvert and loner making it very difficult to find true friends. I just kept to myself through study, work or hobbies most of the time. I have found satisfaction in creativity and thinking, rather than reaching out to find people in a social atmosphere. A few of my real friends through the years included Andy G., Bob K., Dennis B., Michael H., Mohammed A. and Jesus C. Many others have been acquaintances or work-related friendships. Unfortunately, as time goes by, you may have lost contact with some of your friends, either through distance or death.

To me, friendship is having a good relationship with someone. I believe the true meaning of friendship is when you consider the other person's well-being to be as valuable as your own.

Friends have respect for each other. A best friend is a person who you value above others in your life, someone you have fun with, someone you trust and someone in whom you confide. They are the first person you call when you get good news or just want to go out for a bite to eat. A true friend is someone who has touched your heart, someone you care for, and who cares for you. They are someone you can do the stupidest things around and always be forgiven. They are someone you'll instantly remember in ten years because they are in your heart and not just your mind. They have the ability to change you, even if they don't. They will be etched in your memories forever.

What a friend we have in Jesus!

Back in 1967 I wrote a poem that describes a feeling of loneliness when an individual has no one as a friend.

The Lone Oak

The squirrels are scampering on my arms
My goods they stop to buy.
But, though they stay so short a time
I know the reason why.

They love the taste of food so sweet
Which only I can give,
They know I'm glad to give to them
The food that makes them live.

It's good to give all that you can
So others may survive.
It makes the heart so full of glee
To know that their alive.

But, why am I so lonely,
While others are so free
To do and go where 'ere they please
On top this big Oak tree?

To people I do furnish shade
In all mid-summer's heat
To rest themselves on my big trunk
For easing their sore feet.

Although the sun and clouds are here
To talk to me today,
There seems to be a missing link
Which shows me the right way,

To know that others have the same
Continual emptiness,
Which lurks inside this big Oak tree
Where birds have made their nest.

CHAPTER 29 - HOUSEHOLDS

The Good Old Days

My twin sisters (2 years younger) and I were born shortly after World War II. My dad drove street car on the Selby-Lake line between Minneapolis and St. Paul. My mom would take me on rides to go shopping; sitting on the street cars' highly varnished yellow basket weave seats.

"The promise is for you and your children and for all who are far off—for all whom the Lord our God will call."
(Acts 2:39)

The milk man would deliver our eggs; and milk in glass bottles sealed with wax-coated cardboard bottle caps. I remember trying to help carry the milk bottles into the house at the age of two, and dropping a bottle on the steps, watching the milk slowly creep across the floor from the screen porch entry to the kitchen door.

I also remember sitting in my highchair refusing to eat, and my mother exclaiming "Come Bozo, come and eat". (Bozo was a neighborhood dog.) This is where one of my sisters' ate egg shells out of the garbage under the kitchen sink, and she would also eat all of the white sand out of the sandbox.

To keep us in the small yard, mom would tie ropes around our waists with the other end tied to the clothesline which allowed us to run back and forth. My parents had told me that, in order to get me to go to sleep, they would tie some clothesline to the handle of the buggy, push me down the short hallway and pull me back until I would fall asleep.

As God tells us in *Ecclesiastes 7:10* "Do not say 'Why were the old days better than these?' and also in *Ecclesiastes 7:14* "When times are good, be happy; but when times are bad, consider: God has made the one as well as the other. Therefore, a man cannot discover anything about his future." The tapestry of life's events make up who we are. God creates memories. Remember things the way they really were, content with things as they are and trust God to take care of the future.

"Do not be deceived: God cannot be mocked. A man reaps what he sows. The one who sows to please his sinful nature, from that nature will reap destruction; the one who sows to please the Spirit, from the Spirit will reap eternal life. Let us not become weary in doing good, for at the proper time we will reap a harvest if we do not give up. Therefore, as we have opportunity, let us do good to all people, especially to those who belong to the family of believers." (Galatians 6:7-10)

The Family Tree

Our entire family – our three children, their spouses, the nine grandchildren, mother-in-law and brother-in-law - all still live in Minnesota, with the exception of one son and family that made their home in Phoenix a few years ago.

Within the past several years, I have been engrossed in the study of my heritage. My curiosity has led me through more than 4,000 individuals in more than 700 families from many countries in the world. (I am confident that my ancestors can be traced back to Adam and Eve, Moses and Noah. Just take a look at the census in the book of *Numbers*.)

It is interesting how the branches and roots of the family are created, the various skills and trades that form the foundation of each family, and the Christian beliefs that are woven into the fabric of each family through many generations. According to *Psalm 78:2-4*, "I will open my mouth with a parable; I will utter hidden things, things from of old-- things we have heard and known, things our ancestors have told us. We will not hide them from their descendants; we will tell the next generation the praiseworthy deeds of the Lord, his power, and the wonders he has done."

We Reap What We Sow

Evil is a product of Satan. For reasons we may not ever fully accept or grasp while living our lives on earth, God allows pain into our lives; biblically, pain is often an indicator that God is alive and attempting to change something about the way we live our lives.

Billy Graham's daughter, Anne, was once interviewed. Jane Clayson asked her "How can God let bad things happen to people?" specifically regarding to the terrorist attack against our nation Sept. 11, 2001. The following is Ms. Graham's response.

"I believe that God is deeply saddened by this, just as we are, but for years we've been telling God to get out of our schools, to get out of our government, and to get out of our lives. And being the gentleman that He is, I believe that He has calmly backed out. How can we expect God to give us His blessing and His protection if we demand that He leave us alone?

Let's see, I think it started when Madeline Murray O'Hare (she was murdered, her body was found recently) complained she didn't want any prayer in our schools, and we said, OK.

Then, someone said you better not read the Bible in school... the Bible that says thou shalt not kill, thou shalt not steal, and love your neighbor as yourself. And we said, OK.

Then, Dr. Benjamin Spock said we shouldn't spank our children when they misbehave because their little personalities would be warped and we might damage their self-esteem. (Dr. Spock's son committed suicide.) And we said, an expert should know what he's talking about, so we said OK.

Then, someone said teachers and principals better not discipline our children when they misbehave. And the school administrators said no faculty member in this school better touch a student when they misbehave because we don't want any bad publicity, and we surely don't want to be sued. (There's a big difference between disciplining and touching, beating, smacking, humiliating, kicking, etc.) And we said, OK.

Then someone said, let's let our daughters have abortions if they want, and they won't even have to tell their parents. And we said, OK.

Then some wise school-board member said, since boys will be boys and they're going to do it anyway, let's give our sons all the condoms they want, so they can have all the fun they desire, and we won't have to tell their parents they got them at school. And we said, OK.

Then some of our top elected officials said it doesn't matter what we do in private as long as we do our jobs. And agreeing with them, we said it doesn't matter to me what anyone, including the President, does in private as long as I have a job and the economy is good.

And then the entertainment industry said, let's make TV shows and movies that promote profanity, violence, and illicit sex. And let's record music that encourages rape, drugs, murder, suicide, and satanic themes. And we said it's just entertainment, it has no adverse effect, and nobody takes it seriously anyway, so go right ahead.

Now we're asking ourselves why our children have no conscience, why they don't know right from wrong, and why it doesn't bother them to kill strangers, their classmates, and themselves. Probably, if we think about it long and hard enough, we can figure it out. I think it has a great deal to do with "WE REAP WHAT WE SOW."

CHAPTER 30 – PEACE, LOVE AND JOY

I PRAY FOR PEACE, LOVE AND JOY IN THEIR HOMES THAT ALL THEIR NEEDS ARE MET.

Healing

During my full-time tenure at the electric company, I had several promotions. The most notable was a management position that allowed my wife to quit work at the same time we built a house. My left arm began to go numb again on a regular basis. We were afraid that the Guillain-Barre syndrome had returned.

"Let the peace of Christ rule in your hearts, since as members of one body you were called to peace. And be thankful." (Colossians 3:15)

After extensive testing, the doctors determined that it was a pinched nerve in my neck instead. They performed two surgeries at the same time. One team removed a small piece of bone on the ilium of my right hip while the other team moved my esophagus out of the way from the front of my neck to fuse this hip bone piece between two vertebrae.

"Peace I leave with you; My peace I give you. I do not give to you as the world gives. Do not let your hearts be troubled and do not be afraid." (John 14:27)

Several weeks of healing with a neck-brace, and I was good as new. (It actually took longer for the hip to heal than it did my neck.)

My wife would force me to walk five blocks to a small coffee shop on a daily basis for breakfast or lunch, just to get the necessary physical therapy exercise. Of course she would come with and give me much encouragement. (Thank you dear.)

"You will keep in perfect peace him whose mind is steadfast, because he trusts in you." (*Isaiah 26:3*) Jesus instructed us, beginning in *Matthew 6:25*, not to worry about our life, especially about such things as food or clothing. He said "Look at the birds of the air; they do not sow or reap or store away in barns, and yet your heavenly Father feeds them. Are you not much more valuable than they? Who of you by worrying can add a single hour to his life?" He also described the lilies of the field dressed in splendor. He then explained, "Seek first His kingdom and His righteousness, and all these things will be given to." - (*Mathew 6:33*)

Rejoice
The natural condition of a person in a relationship with God is joy. Kevin G. Harney explains that from the Old Testament to the New, the Bible declares this message: in the good and hard times, those who walk closely with God can and should experience life-transforming joy.

"On the last and greatest day of the Feast, Jesus stood and said in a loud voice, "If anyone is thirsty, let him come to Me and drink. Whoever believes in Me, as the Scripture has said, streams of living water will flow from within him."
(John 7:37-38)

"And my God will meet all your needs according to His glorious riches in Christ Jesus."
(Philippians 4:19)

The words joy, rejoice, rejoicing, and joyful appear more than three hundred and fifty times in the Bible.

Some of these passages talk about people facing a time of joylessness, but it is clear that it is not the natural and ongoing condition of a Christian's heart. God is ready to let joy freely flow into our hearts.

Thanksgiving

"I will praise the name of God with a song, and will magnify Him with thanksgiving." (*Psalm 69:30*) Thanksgiving, or Thanksgiving Day, is a public holiday celebrated on the fourth Thursday of November in the United States. It originated as a harvest festival. Thanksgiving has been celebrated nationally since 1789, after Congress requested a proclamation by George Washington. It has been celebrated as a federal holiday since 1864, when, during the American Civil War, President Abraham Lincoln proclaimed a national day of "Thanksgiving and Praise to our beneficent Father who dwelleth in the Heavens," to be celebrated on the last Thursday in November.

"He who did not spare His own Son, but gave Him up for us all—how will He not also, along with Him, graciously give us all things?" (Romans 8:32)

"And He is not served by human hands, as if He needed anything, because He Himself gives all men life and breath and everything else." (Acts 17:25)

"Do not be like them, for your Father knows what you need before you ask Him." (Matthew 6:8)

The event that Americans call the "First Thanksgiving" was celebrated by the Pilgrims after their first harvest in the New World in October 1621. This feast lasted three days, and—as accounted by attendee Edward Winslow—it was attended by 90 Native Americans and 53 Pilgrims. The colonists were accustomed to celebrating days of prayer thanking God for blessings such as military victory or the end of a drought.

Setting aside time to give thanks for blessings, and holding feasts to celebrate a harvest, are both practices that predate the European settlement of North America. The first documented thanksgiving services in territory belonging to the United States were conducted by Spaniards and the French in the 16th century. Thanksgiving services were routine in the Commonwealth of Virginia as early as 1607. In 1619, 38 English settlers arrived at Berkeley Hundred in Charles City County, Virginia.

The London Company charter specifically required "that the day of our ships arrival at the place assigned... in the land of Virginia shall be yearly and perpetually kept holy as a day of thanksgiving to Almighty God." Three years later, after the Indian massacre of 1622, the Berkeley Hundred site and other outlying locations were abandoned and colonists moved their celebration to Jamestown and other more secure spots.

1 Timothy 2:1-2 "I urge, then, first of all, that petitions, prayers, intercession and thanksgiving be made for all people, for kings and all those in authority, that we may live peaceful and quiet lives in all godliness and holiness."

CHAPTER 31 - EYES

I PRAY THAT EVERY EYE CAN SEE THERE IS NO PROBLEM, CIRCUMSTANCE, OR SITUATION GREATER THAN GOD.

Circumstances

For a few years, I had been diagnosed with severe emphysema and chronic obstructive pulmonary disease (C.O.P.D.).

"For nothing is impossible with God." (Luke 1:37)

COPD is a chronic progressive lung disease, where the lungs are damaged, making it hard to breathe. In COPD, the airways are partly obstructed, making it difficult to get air in and out. Breathing in lung irritants, like air pollution, dust, or chemicals, over a long period of time contribute to COPD.

"Come to Me, all you who are weary and burdened, and I will give you rest." (Matthew 11:28)

In *Ephesians 1:18* we read "I pray that the eyes of your heart may be enlightened in order that you may know the hope to which He has called you, the riches of His glorious inheritance in His holy people." What great hope He gives us!

It is very difficult to walk distances longer than 100 feet without having to stop and catch my breath. I am very sensitive to candles, perfumes, fragrance shampoos and laundry detergent, fireplace and tobacco smoke, mold, and pet hair. My lungs and chest hurt from the pressure when it rains, when it is cold outside, in the wind, at higher elevations above 2500 feet, in swimming pools or even laying on my stomach. High humidity or dew points as well as a high AQI (air quality index) over 50 make it very hard to breath. My best weather days are dry and warm.

"The Lord works out everything for His own ends— even the wicked for a day of disaster." (Proverbs 16:4)

The airway in the lungs branch out like an upside-down tree, and at the end of each branch are many small, balloon-like air sacs called alveoli (al-VEE-uhl-EYE). In healthy people, each airway is clear and open. The air sacs are small and dainty, and both the airways and air sacs are elastic and springy. When you breathe in, each air sac fills up with air like a small balloon; when you breathe out, the balloon deflates and the air goes out.

"But I am like an olive tree flourishing in the house of God; I trust in God's unfailing love for ever and ever. I will praise You forever for what You have done; in Your name I will hope, for Your name is good. I will praise You in the presence of Your saints." (Psalm 52:8-9)

In COPD, the airways and air sacs lose their shape and become floppy. Less air gets in and less air goes out because the airways and air sacs lose their elasticity (like an old rubber band), the walls between many of the air sacs are permanently destroyed, the walls of the airways become thick and inflamed (swollen), and cells in the airways make more mucus (sputum) than usual, which tends to clog the airways.

You cannot repair the damage caused by this disease and it becomes very difficult to cough up the mucus during an exacerbation. After many prayers, God directed us to the dry climate of Phoenix.

During my physical in 2007, the doctor found a lesion on my right lung. After several tests, they were 80% certain it was lung cancer. (My mother died of lung cancer and my dad had emphysema and diabetes.) However, before they would do surgery, they wanted to do a lung biopsy.

Our pastor drove my wife and I to the hospital for the procedure. After a short prayer, he left us there. (He admitted later that he thought the results would be cancer.) A very close friend brought us home. The results were NOT cancer. Apparently, from many years of getting pneumonia during the Minnesota winter months, I had developed scar tissue on my lung. Talk about miracles and blessings. Praise the Lord! Since then I have had a number of lung nodules, each being benign thus far. I have named them 'CiCi', 'Sputnik', 'Leftie', "Top Hat" and "Oscar".

God has kept me strong through each of these health issues. He has taught me to stay uplifted so that I may have words of encouragement for others.

Don't give up
I read a story a while ago and felt it appropriate to share in this chapter. I couldn't help but feel a sense of security and protection as I reflected back on 'Chapter 2 – Creation' in this book, and the many other chapters found within this book of petitions. Perhaps you too can find some solace in this story.

One day I decided to quit. I quit my job, my relationship, my spirituality. I wanted to quit my life. I went to the woods to have one last talk with God.

"God", I asked, "Can you give me one good reason not to quit?" His answer surprised me.

"Look around", He said. "Do you see the fern and the bamboo?" "Yes", I replied. "When I planted the fern and the bamboo seeds, I took very good care of them. I gave them light. I gave them water. The fern quickly grew from the earth. Its brilliant green covered the floor. Yet nothing came from the bamboo seed. But I did not quit on the bamboo.

In the second year the Fern grew more vibrant and plentiful. And again, nothing came from the bamboo seed. But I did not quit on the bamboo. He said. "In year three there was still nothing from the bamboo seed. But I would not quit. In year four, again, there was nothing from the bamboo seed. I would not quit." He said.

"Then in the fifth year a tiny sprout emerged from the earth. Compared to the fern it was seemingly small and insignificant...But just 6 months later the bamboo rose to over 100 feet tall. It had spent the five years growing roots. Those roots made it strong and gave it what it needed to survive.

I would not give any of my creations a challenge it could not handle." He asked me. "Did you know, my child, that all this time you have been struggling, you have actually been growing roots?" "I would not quit on the bamboo. I will never quit on you."

"Don't compare yourself to others." He said. "The bamboo had a different purpose than the fern. Yet they both make the forest beautiful." "Your time will come", God said to me. "You will rise high." "How high should I rise?" I asked. "How high will the bamboo rise?" He asked in return. "As high as it can?" I questioned. "Yes." He said, "Give me glory by rising as high as you can."

I left the forest and brought back this story. I hope these words can help you see that God will never give up on you. **Never, Never, Never Give up.**

Prayer is not an option but an opportunity. Don't tell the Lord how big the problem is, tell the problem how Great the Lord is!

Strength

Brother Yun expressed that challenges in your life are real. If you will learn to praise Jesus Christ regardless of your circumstances, you will find inner freedom and joy, and you will have the strength to overcome whatever you are faced with. The joy of the Lord is such a key, because Nehemiah said, "The joy of the Lord is your strength" (*Nehemiah 8:10*).

If you have allowed the devil to steal the joy of the Lord from you, then you will feel weak and powerless. But when the joy of the Lord returns, you will be strong! If you feel defeated, then "strengthen the feeble hands, steady the knees that give way; say to those with fearful hearts, 'Be strong, do not fear; your God will come'" (*Isaiah 35:3–4*). It is in the very nature of our God to help the oppressed (see *Psalm 146:7–8*).

Lura Van Wormer Bertram once said "Encouragement is the oxygen that keeps us running through the challenges life presents. Listen to one another so you learn the things that encourage one another. Then take the time and energy to do those things. Encourage one another every day."

CHAPTER 32 - BATTLES

EVERY BATTLE IS IN YOUR HANDS FOR YOU TO FIGHT.

You haven't seen, heard, or imagined all of the amazing things that God has in store for you. Believe today that things are changing in your favor. God's done it in the past, and He will do it again in the future.

"All those gathered here will know that it is not by sword or spear that the Lord saves; for the battle is the Lord, and He will give all of you into our hands." (1 Samuel 17:47)

Joel Olsteen recently said "God has armed you with strength for every battle. He said no weapon formed against you will ever prosper." (*Isaiah 54:17*) In *1 Samuel 17:45* David said to the Philistine, "You come against me with sword and spear and javelin, but I come against you in the name of the Lord Almighty, the God of the armies of Israel, whom you have defied."

It is exciting to read of the many victories that God's people won in the Bible. However, sadly, they did not emerge victorious in every battle they fought. Sometimes Israel won. Sometimes it was the Philistines. Occasionally, when Israel won the immediate battle, there was sin in the camp that caused future defeats.

"Do not let your hearts be troubled. Trust in God; trust also in Me." (John 14:1)

Here are 8 battles in the Bible that you should remember. Some are very famous (Jericho, David and Goliath) while others are lesser known (Philistines capturing the Ark).

David and Goliath

Probably the best known battle in the Bible is when the shepherd boy David fought against the well trained soldier named Goliath. They met when David came to bring supplies to his brothers who were engaged in battle as soldiers with Israel against the Philistines. Goliath came to the front lines and declared that he would go one-on-one with anyone who dared to face him. Goliath challenged the veracity of the faith of Israel in their God. Goliath did not believe in Israel's God and therefore mocked God because of the fear that the people had for Goliath. (*1 Samuel 17:8-11*)

David took the challenge to fight Goliath. King Saul offered his royal armor to David for the battle. David said that he did not need those things to fight the giant. He would trust in the God of Israel who had saved him from attacks by a lion and a bear. This same God would save David from Goliath. (*1 Samuel 17:32-39*)

David carefully chose five stones from a stream and charged towards Goliath. Goliath was amazed that a young boy would come so bravely towards him. David fitted a stone in his sling and sent it towards Goliath. God guided the rock which struck Goliath between the eyes. David took the giant sword of the fallen warrior and cut off Goliath's head. (*1 Samuel 17:40-51*) The Philistines fled and Israel pursued. God won a great victory in Israel that day through the hand of a young man who trusted in his God.

Jericho

Joshua led the children of Israel back to the Jordan River to cross into the Promised Land after wandering in the wilderness for 40 years. Their first obstacle was the city of Jericho. This large walled city was formidable, but through the work of spies they learned that the people of Jericho were scared of Israel. (*Joshua 1-2*)

Joshua received his marching orders from an appearance of the "Captain of the Lord's Host." This may have been an appearance of God personally to bring the message to Joshua. The message was that the Hebrew military would march around the city once a day for six days. On the seventh day they would march around seven times. (*Joshua 5:13-6:5*)

Following God's plan, the children of Israel defeated the city of Jericho. After they marched around the city according to their instructions, the walls fell down. Israel entered the city and took the city as their first victory in the new territory God had promised to them several hundred years before. (*Joshua 6:6-27*)

Ai

Immediately following the battle of Jericho the Israelites went up to the city of Ai. The whole army did not go because it was a much smaller city than Jericho. However, they were turned away by the might of this small town. Thirty-six Hebrews died in the battle that should have been an easy win for them. (*Joshua 7:3-5*)

God revealed to Joshua that there was sin in the camp. A man named Achan had taken gold, silver and garments from Jericho. (*Joshua 7:20-21*) According to God's plan, all the spoils from Jericho were to be dedicated to God. After that, God planned to allow the children of Israel to keep all future spoils. However, when Achan stole that which should have been dedicated to God he brought judgment on the people.

After that, Achan and all that he owned were stoned and burned. (*Joshua 7:25*) Israel once again marched against the city of Ai. Again a partial army presented themselves to Ai. When the men of Ai came out against Israel, the Israelites fled in retreat. But this time their retreat was a tactical move to pull the men out of the city so that the rest of the army could enter Ai unabated and take the city. (*Joshua 8:3-8*)

Philistines Take the Ark

Israel battled the Philistines often in the Bible. In *1 Samuel 4* the Philistines overcame Israel and killed about 4,000 men. (*1 Samuel 4:2*) Israel went to seek out the Ark of the Covenant from Shiloh where it was located because they were convinced that the presence of the Ark would protect them in battle. (*1 Samuel 4:3-5*) They trusted in the Ark more than in the God of the Ark.

When the Ark arrived in the camp, the Israelites cheered so loudly that the Philistines wondered what was taking place. They learned that the Ark had come into the camp. Though the Philistines had never experienced God's presence directly, they had heard stories. And the stories frightened them. They recounted to one another how that God had done mighty works for Israel when He led them from Egypt. Not wanting to become servants of Israel, the Philistines fought even harder. They killed 30,000 of Israel's infantry. (*1 Samuel 4:10*) Besides losing the Ark, the son's of Eli, the high priest, were killed in the battle. (*1 Samuel 4:2-11*)

Again, Israel trusted in the mere presence of the Ark. What they needed was the presence of God.

Gideon

God sent an angel to speak to Gideon who was gathering wheat. Israel had been surrounded by the army of the Midianites and cut off from supplies. Gideon was working diligently when he got the message that God wanted him to lead an army against the enemy. Gideon was humbled by the personal request from God, but agreed to let God use him. (*Judges 6:12-16*)

Gideon gathered all the men he could to go against Midian. His army numbered 32,000 men. But God said that was too many. Gideon invited all those who were afraid to go back home without any repercussions. He was probably quite disappointed when 22,000 of them turned and walked away. God said that the 10,000 were too many. (*Judges 7:3*)

God instructed Gideon to take the remaining men to a place to get a drink. Most fell on their stomachs to drink deeply from the water. A few scooped the water to their mouths so that they could keep their eyes open for any enemies. God told Gideon that those men who were vigilant were the men who were to go against Midian. (*Judges 7:5-7*) While it was good that Gideon was given the best of the soldiers, they only numbered 300 men. If he was disappointed before, he was even more so now. But God assured Gideon that the battle would be won by the Lord and not by the men. God did not want anyone thinking that Gideon and his men won the battle. They were merely tools in God's hand.

Standing in the hills over the camp of the 135,000 man army of the Midianites must have been frightening. However, God told Gideon to go down into the camp and listen to a couple men tell about a dream.

One man said that he dreamed that a large loaf of barley rolled down the hill and crushed the camp. The other man said that it was a vision that Gideon would trample them. They did not know that Gideon and a servant were sitting outside their tent listening to the conversation. Gideon returned to the camp encouraged about the battle. (*Judges 7:9-15*)

Gideon equipped the men with trumpets, clay pots and lanterns. At Gideon's signal they broke their pots and blew their horns. The men of Midian were startled awake with all the noise. Confused, they began fighting one another. Of those who escaped (only 15,000), Gideon was able to capture them in the chase that followed. (*Judges 8:10-12*)

There was no question that God gave the 300-man army of Israel victory over the 135,000-man army of Midian.

Saul Against the Amalekites
Samuel gave the battle plan to King Saul for the fight against Amalek. The armies of Israel were to battle the Amelekites and King Agag to the death. There were not to be any men or animals

left standing. (*1 Samuel 15:3*) Saul led an army of 210,000 men. But Saul and the people did not obey the command of God. They spared King Agag and the best of the animals. (*1 Samuel 15:9, 14-15*) These animals were supposedly for a sacrifice to God.

When the prophet Samuel found out that God's orders were not obeyed, he became angry with Saul. His excuse was that it was the people who had made the decision and that the animals were saved for a good cause. (*1 Samuel 15:15*) However, Samuel told Saul that God would rather have obedience than sacrifice. (*1 Samuel 15:22*) Samuel called for King Agag to be brought before him. The Bible says that Agag came into the presence of Samuel cautiously, but hopeful that his life might be spared. (*1 Samuel 15:32*) Within moments Samuel declared that as Agag had caused many women to be childless, his mother was about to lose her own child. At that point Samuel cut Agag into pieces. (*1 Samuel 15:33*)

Battle of Armageddon
After the rapture of the church and the great tribulation, Jesus Himself will lead an army at the battle of Armageddon. Christ and His army will descend on white horses to do battle against the beast, the false prophet and the kings of the earth. (*Revelation 19:11-14*) Christ and His armies fight with swords and emerge victorious. The beast and false prophet are taken and cast into the lake of fire. (*Revelation 19:20*) Those who remain are slain. The birds of the field will feast on their flesh.

Jacob Wrestles With God
(*Genesis 32:22-32*) The appearance of the angels in verses 1 and 2 sets the tone for the entire chapter. From a divine point of view chapter 32 was the turning point of Jacob's spiritual life. Jacob had been a bargainer, even with God, up to this time. In *Genesis 28,* after the vision of the heavenly ladder, Jacob made a vow, but it was much more of a bargain with God than a surrender to Him.

Then Jacob made a vow, saying, "If God will be with me and will keep me on this journey that I take, and will give me food to eat and garments to wear, and I return to my father's house in safety, then the LORD will be my God. And this stone, which I have set up as a pillar, will be God's house; and of all that Thou dost give me I will surely give a tenth to Thee." (*Genesis 28:20-22*)

To me, this was a bargain with God. In return for God's presence, protection, and provision, Jacob would let God be his God. Of all that God gave to him in the form of wealth, Jacob would return ten percent. In effect, Jacob has made God his agent and offered Him the normal fee. What a far cry from what a man's response to the living God should be!

All of Jacob's deceitful practices which we have seen over the years of his life are the result of a fundamental misconception. Jacob felt that spiritual blessings were to be secured by carnal methods and means. Jacob rightly believed that God had promised to make him, not Esau, the heir of promise with the rights of the first-born. He valued this blessing while Esau despised it. What he did not yet know was that he did not have to connive and scheme in order to obtain the promised blessings of God. The encounter which Jacob will have with the Angel of Jehovah will correct this error and will instruct Jacob as to how and why spiritual blessings must be obtained through spiritual means.

The struggle was not a dream or a nightmare. Never has a man awakened from such a "dream" with a limp! And it was a struggle which God Himself initiated: "Then Jacob was left alone, and a man wrestled with him until daybreak." (*Genesis 32:24*)

Summary
Some of the other battles include the Battle of Mount Zemaraim, the Battle of Aphek, the Battle of Siddim, the Battle of Michmash, the Battle of Refidim, the Sack of Jerusalem, the Siege of Lachish, the Battle of the Waters of Merom, Jeroboam's Revolt and the Battle of Zephath.

Not all the battles that Israel and God's people fought ended in victory. It was only when they obeyed the Lord and trusted in God did they emerge victorious. In our own lives today we face battles. Not on a field with swords and spears, but in our hearts and minds.

We can only be victorious if we are obedient to what God has revealed to us. So many times people complain that they aren't seeing victories in their lives, yet they ignore the fact that they are not being obedient. Or maybe they are trusting in the Lord today, but are suffering the consequences of past disobedience. We may have forgiveness of sins, but that does not mean that all the consequences will be taken away from us.

God wants us to live victorious Christian lives. But for us to win our daily battles we need to follow the One who leads us.

CONCLUSION

I PRAY THAT I WILL CONTINUE TO RECEIVE YOUR LOVE IN MY HEART AND TO SHARE THIS LOVE WITH EVERY ONE THAT I ENCOUNTER TODAY. IN JESUS PRECIOUS NAME. AMEN!

Paul wrote to the church in Philippi, "This is my prayer: that your love may abound more and more in knowledge and depth of insight, so that you may be able to discern what is best and may be pure and blameless until the day of Christ." (*Philippians 1:9-10*). He also wrote with the repeated use of the words "joy" and "rejoice" throughout this letter. Paul had the ability to find joy and contentment in any circumstance. Notice that Paul held up Christ as the model for Christians to follow and included a beautiful psalm of praise to Jesus. (*Philippians 2:5–11*)

The Apostle John further calls for Christians to live in a godly manner: turning from sin, obeying God's commands, showing love to other believers, abandoning worldly glory and holding fast to orthodox teachings about Jesus Christ. "This is how God showed His love among us: He sent His one and only Son into the world that we might live through Him." (*1 John 4:9*)

"Greater love has no one than this that He lay down His life for His friends." (John 15:13)

"But God demonstrates His own love for us in this: While we were still sinners, Christ died for us." (Romans 5:8)

"But encourage one another daily, as long as it is called Today, so that none of you may be hardened by sin's deceitfulness." (Hebrews 3:13)

May you continue to share His love with every one that you encounter each and every day as it is written in *2 Corinthians 13:14* - "May the grace of the Lord Jesus Christ, and the love of God, and the fellowship of the Holy Spirit be with you all." And remember, "So whether you eat or drink or whatever you do, do it all for the glory of God." (*1 Corinthians 10:31*)

So Who Is Jesus

Jesus is one part of the Triune God. The Christian doctrine of the Trinity (Latin: *Trinitas*, lit. 'triad', from *trinus*, "threefold") holds that God is three persons—the Father, the Son (Jesus Christ), and the Holy Spirit—as "one God in three Divine Persons". Christian beliefs about God are expressed in the doctrine of the Trinity. This doctrine is unique to Christianity. The Trinity is a way of describing the three ways of being God – God the Father, God the Son and God the Holy Spirit. We believe in one God the Father, maker of heaven and earth, His Son and the Holy Ghost as One Divine being.

The Triune God (God the Father, God the Son and God the Holy Spirit) is present in specific references in the Bible: The baptism of Jesus is described in the gospels of *Matthew*, *Mark* and *Luke*. *John*'s gospel does not directly describe Jesus' baptism.

"Therefore go and make disciples of all nations, baptizing them in the name of the Father and of the Son and of the Holy Spirit, and teaching them to obey everything I have commanded you. And surely I am with you always, to the very end of the age." (Matthew 28:19-20)

"You may ask Me for anything in My Name, and I will do it." (John 14:14)

Luke records that Jesus was praying when Heaven was opened and the Holy Spirit descended on Him. *Luke* clarifies that the Spirit descended in the "bodily form" of a dove, as opposed to merely "descending like" a dove. In the gospels, the accounts of *Luke* and *Mark* record the voice (God the Father) as addressing Jesus by saying "You are my beloved Son, in whom I am well pleased", while in *Matthew* the voice addresses the crowd "This is my beloved Son, in whom I am well pleased" (*Matthew 3:13–17; Mark 1:9–11; Luke 3:21–23*).

From the beginning of creation in *Genesis* to the end of times in *Revelation*, God refers to Himself as "us" or "our" and thus describes the doctrine of the Trinity. The word trinity comes from "tri" meaning three and "unity" meaning one. God is three distinct individuals - God the Father, the Son Jesus, and the Holy Spirit - in one true God. *Corinthians* talks a lot about the trinity. For example, "May the grace of the Lord Jesus Christ, and the love of God, and the fellowship of the Holy Spirit be with you all." (*2 Corinthians 13:14*) In the book of *Luke* we read "The angel answered, "The Holy Spirit will come on you, and the power of the Most High will overshadow you. So the holy one to be born will be called the Son of God." (*Luke 1:35*) And in the book of Matthew we read "Therefore go and make disciples of all nations, baptizing them in the name of the Father and of the Son and of the Holy Spirit," (*Matthew 28:19*)

To get a better understanding, take a look at Jesus' relationship to the Trinity.

God the Father founded the earth and established the heavens (*Proverbs 3:19*), formed man from the dust of the ground, (*Genesis 2:7*), and breathed into man the breath of life, (*Genesis 2:7*). He has been called a Wonderful Counselor. (*Isaiah 9:6*) People who listen to Him are safe and don't fear evil. (*Proverbs 1:33*) God encompasses the entire breadth and length of knowledge, wisdom and understanding. (*Proverbs 2:6*) His Word is so powerful; it has been described as being a lamp unto your feet and a lamp unto your path. (*Psalm 119:105*) He can tell you all of the secrets of your heart. (*Psalm 44:21*)

Jesus can be found in *Ephesians 1:20,* and called directly in *Romans 10:13.* His name is Jesus Christ. Many call Him Lord. He redeemed man from the curse of the law, (*Galatians 3:13*) and blessings of the Abrahamic Covenant comes upon your life through Jesus. (*Galatians 3:14*)

Jesus, God's Son, came to earth in human form for a specific purpose (*Luke 2:49*), without ever being disobedient or disrespectful. The Spirit of God is with Him. (*Matthew 3:15-17*)

Jesus empowered the poor so that they would no longer be poor, healed the brokenhearted, set captives free, healed the sick, miraculously fed the poor, raised the dead and restored sight to the blind. (*Luke 4:18*) He has the authority, ability and power to cleanse you of your sins. (*I John 1:7-9*) In Him are hid all of the treasures of wisdom and knowledge. (*Colossians 2:3*) He laid down His life so that you may live. (*II Corinthians 5:15*) He defeated the archenemy of God and mankind and made a show of them openly. (*Colossians 2:15*) Believers and followers worldwide will testify to His divine healings, salvation, deliverance, miracles, restoration and supernatural guidance.

He will properly direct your paths (*Proverbs 3:5-6*), and lead you into everlasting life. (*John 6:47*) **When can He be part of your life?** Time is of the essence. (*Hebrews 3:15*)

"Because of the Lord's great love we are not consumed, for His compassions never fail. They are new every morning; great is Your faithfulness." (*Lamentations 3:22-23*)

Did you remember to pray today? God didn't forget to wake you up this morning.

References and Further Reading

Rest: Living in Sabbath Simplicity by Keri Wyatt Kent

You Were Made for More: The Life You Have, the Life God Wants You to Have by Jim Cymbala

A Little Guide to Christian Spirituality: Three Dimensions of Life with God by Glen G. Scorgie

The Sacred Echo: Hearing God's Voice In Every Area Of Your Life by Margaret Feinberg

How Churches And Leaders Can Get It and Keep It by Craig Groeschel

The Seven Desires of Every Heart by Mark & Debra Laaser

I Stand at the Door and Knock: Meditations by the Author of *The Hiding Place* by Corrie Ten Boom

Flowing Streams: Journeys Of A Life Well Lived by Stuart Briscoe

The Tender Words of God by Ann Spangler

The Relationship Principles of Jesus by Tom Holladay

Soul Revolution: How Imperfect People Become All God Intended by John Burke

When The Game Is Over It All Goes Backin The Box by John Ortberg

New Women's Devotional Bible

Seismic Shifts: The Little Changes That Make a Big Difference in Your Life by Kevin G. Harney

Living Water by Brother Yun

The Laminins by Peter Elkblom and Rupert Timpl

ABOUT THE AUTHOR

A native of Minneapolis, Minnesota, Dave acknowledges that God has blessed him in so many ways during his life journey. God watches over him physically, mentally, financially and spiritually every day. God could have taken his life at a very early age during a car accident, but God protected him. God blessed him with loving Christian parents. He blessed him with the opportunity to attend a Christian parochial school, academy and college. God healed his 'physical heart condition' and placed his heart in the middle of his chest to remind him where his heart should always be – God centered.

God spoke to Dave twice. First, with a calling into the ministry and second, to go into the world and share His great news. God asked him to share his family values, skills and faith in Sunday School teaching, Church choir, Easter plays, Christmas pageants, outdoor summertime musicals, youth counseling, Cub Scout Master, Boy Scout Leader, Jaycees, coaching soccer, baseball and track, family guitar sing-alongs and camping.

God gave Dave patience during many stressful times. He allowed Dave to have severe emphysema and C.O.P.D., but assured him that the nodules and lesions on his lungs were not cancer. He even gave Dave a light tap on his heart with a mild heart attack to remind him that God is always present in his life. Dave and his wife are now retired and live in Phoenix, Arizona.

Made in the USA
Columbia, SC
29 March 2018